# Forward
**by Ray Illingworth C.B...**
**Former Yorkshire and ...**

When Roger asked me to write a forward for the book he was writing regarding an on-running dispute with Hillsborough Golf Club, I said I would like to read the book myself before deciding.

I personally have had many disputes with committees, the first being when I left Yorkshire CCC in the sixties and I would liken Brian Sellers, the then Chairman of Yorkshire CCC to the Mr Jack Timms in Roger's book, one man making all the decisions and not in the best interest of the Club.

Having read Roger's book it is truly an amazing story and an experience neither him nor his family should have had to put up with. If this book opens the eyes of some of the members of Hillsborough G.C. and makes sure that this never happens again to anyone else then it will have served its purpose.

Don't forget Roger is not doing this for financial gain. Any profits will go to Sheffield Hospitals.

Having played golf in Spain with Roger I sincerely hope he found it more enjoyable than Hillsborough Golf Club.

*Ray Illingworth*

# Preface

As a result of what has happened over the last few years I have lost friends, people I trusted and who I believed trusted me. Friendships spanning fifty years or more since school days have crumbled. My life and those of my wife and son have changed because of it.

I have felt driven to expose the shameful actions directed against me and my family by people intent only on covering up their own wrongdoings. A great deal of hurt and discomfort has been placed upon us, not to mention the underhand activities generated at those who have loyally supported me throughout my ordeal, for no other reason than they could see what was happening was wrong and had the courage to stand up and be counted.

In any case, I hope you enjoy the book and in the words of Ray Illingworth ....'if this never happens again to anyone else, then it will have served its purpose.'

**Roger Baker**

To Nick.
Hope you enjoy the book.
Cheers.
Roger + June.

# Hillsborough Golf Club

# DEFINITELY NOT PAR FOR THE COURSE

by Roger Baker

Published in Great Britain in 2005
By Baker–Roger

ISBN 0 9550813 0 0

Printed in England by Slater Print Group, Sheffield.

# Contents

# Chapter 1

# Over My Dead Body

If you had asked me at the turn of the millennium if I had any intention of writing a book I would have looked at you as if you had gone stark staring mad. I am a builder not a writer and I doubt I would have had much to write about. I feel far more comfortable with bricks and mortar than I do with switching on a word processor but circumstances change and it is these strange circumstances that form the basis of this story; one man's attempt if you like to get justice and the obstacles that are thrown in your way by people who are only interested in themselves and maintaining the status quo because it suits them. If this sounds a rather bitter way to open proceedings then so be it. There have been many times over the last few years when I have been too angry, upset or both to sleep and the same has applied, and still does, to my wife June. She and my son, Ricky have been affected by the story I am going to tell just as much as I and in some respects even more.

Up until this time I had led a fairly normal life and certainly not one I would want to put into a book. I was born and bred in Sheffield, where I still live. As a child I lived in Heeley a typical Sheffield neighbourhood. I have two brothers, Tony and David and two sisters, Betty and Carol. For a while we moved to Derbyshire living in Curber before I left school at fifteen to serve as an apprentice bricklayer at Eyam in Derbyshire. By the age of sixteen I had moved back to Sheffield and my old haunts in Heeley spending most of my spare time knocking about the local coffee shop.

Sheffield has various claims to fame. It is England's fourth largest city and is still deservedly well remembered for its steel and cutlery making industries. Over a third of the city lies inside the Peak National Park, making Sheffield one of the greenest cities in Europe. It boasts two leading universities as well as the Meadowhall shopping mall which attracts 30 million visitors a year. On a more historical note Sheffield FC, an amateur club is the world's oldest football club whilst Hallam FC, their traditional rivals have the world's oldest football ground. More recently however it has become well known for the high grossing movie The Full Monty starring Robert Carlyle.

Anyway that is where I have lived for most of my life. In 1966 I married my wife June and we have two sons Ricky and Russell. Like both June and I, Ricky is also a keen golfer and I have devoted a chapter of this book to his dealings with Hillsborough Golf Club as indeed I have with my wife June. As I write this I cannot help feeling that maybe Russell was the wisest one by taking no interest at all in the game. Both of my boys are now in their thirties but still live and work locally.

When June and I married we bought a row of four tiny terraced houses in another suburb of Sheffield called Dronfield for the princely sum of £500 for the lot. One of the houses was vacant the other three tenanted but all identical in that they had no bathroom or inside toilet. This was the start of my renovation business. We moved into the vacant one and the other three were rented out for a nominal sum. After Russell was born we moved and renovated a terraced house in the Darnall area of Sheffield, letting my old house to the parents of my close friend John Hall. John I am afraid is very much an important part of this whole sorry tale and I will not go into further detail here since as you will see as I proceed with the story that my friendship with John has come to a sudden halt. Anyway I let the house to John's parents for fifteen shillings (75 pence) a week.

In 1975 I bought a derelict building in Loxley and renovated it into a house. We have lived there ever since. Of course if things had turned out differently we may not have been living there any longer but thereby hangs this tale.

Prior to the purchase of my current home the council compulsorily purchased the four houses I owned in Dronfield for £2,000. Finances in those days were rather tight as work in the building trade was a bit thin on the ground and to see us through I tried my hand at a number of different jobs, first doing a stint at window cleaning and for a while I worked, delivering coal. June helped out by working early evenings as cashier at the cinema. We were helped considerably by two things, June managed to get a full time job with Midland Bank (now HSBC) and the government started giving out grants for renovating older houses. I jumped on this bandwagon and assisted by June's full-time wage we managed in time to build up a small portfolio of properties concentrating on purchasing tenanted houses. By the 1980's we were able to buy an apartment in Spain and I also took up golf.

June and I had always taken a keen interest in golf. We played municipal courses whenever we had the chance and always planned to join a club and take up the sport seriously as soon as work commitments would allow. My brother David was already a member at Hillsborough Golf Club and I joined in the late 1980's, June joined about two years later and Ricky a couple of years after that.

The club is situated about four miles outside Sheffield City centre and is based on moor land less than a mile from my own house.

Hillsborough Golf Club is no different from many other private clubs in the United Kingdom. It is run as a limited company by the members for the members with visitors and guests being allowed to play under certain restrictions. The club operates with an elected Committee headed by the President who is selected by his predecessors, as is the Club Captain.

Hillsborough is a wonderful golf course and we made some good friends amongst the other members. We attended Captain's and President's days, charity events and so forth and took part in all the club competitions, especially mixed and social affairs. In short as a family we supported the club as much as anyone and were very happy there.

It was not until the summer of 1999 that things slowly but remorselessly began to change.

Around this time the golf club was not as successful behind the scenes as first impressions might give. In recent times there had been several disputes and the club had on occasion received some bad press. Money however was now the major talking point. Concerns had been raised by the committee that the clubhouse and other facilities were not up to scratch.

The club nevertheless possessed land that was not an integral part of the course, a plot of land on Stubbing Lane which adjoined the fifth fairway. There had been nothing there for many years except an old building known as the potting shed, which apparently dated back over 100 years and it was a logical development that the club should seek to raise funding by attempting to sell off the land. As a golfer and builder, I went ahead and made a proposal to bid for the land with a view to building my own house there.

It is most unlikely that the majority of golfers at Hillsborough, including myself, had previously been aware that the plot of land actually existed, since it was hidden by trees adjoining the fifth fairway but exist it certainly did and a house there would have backed onto existing property on Stubbing Lane and overlooked the golf course itself.

Surprisingly enough, despite the club being seriously in need of funds, it had been decided by the committee that bidding for the land was to be open solely to club members and each bid was to be submitted to the club through the Secretary and placed on the club notice board. Whilst this may seem somewhat archaic, this was the procedure and one that I followed. On 5th August 1999, I wrote to the Secretary making a formal offer to purchase the land for the sum of £77,000.

The committee planned to hold an Extraordinary General Meeting on 10th September 1999, at which they intended to seek permission from the members to sanction the sale of the land. The Club President, Jack Timms, confirmed this to me in a letter dated 17th August with the following proviso:

*"Assuming that the approval is forthcoming the Committee then intend to conclude negotiations with one of the interested purchasers and to enter a Contract with the purchaser for the sale of the land, subject to the granting of planning consent for the conversion of the buildings on the land to residential use."*

Restrictions were also put in place including contract timings, as well as stating that all fees and other expenses in connection with the application were to be funded by the purchaser.

At the EGM it was immediately voted in favour of the proposed sale of the land at Stubbing Lane. Strangely enough my offer of £77,000 made over a month before had still not been put on the notice board and the only bid still showing was the one of £75,000 made by another member and builder, Philip Willers. Neither did the President, Mr Timms mention to club members at the meeting that an increased offer for the land had been received, which I did find a little strange at the time.

Proposals had also been made to consider the overall ways of funding improvements to the Club. A considerable amount of work was needed to maintain the fabric of the clubhouse; wiring, heating, new windows and so forth and to finance the work each member would support the scheme by way of a £100 debenture.

In addition, Development Plans had been put forward by the committee which involved extensive new building works, not least of which was the proposed erection of a large new professional shop. The Treasurer at the time outlined that as well as a marked increase in member's subscriptions; a proposed mortgage of several hundred thousand pounds would be required to fund the suggested work.

Unlike many private golf clubs, Hillsborough is not a club made up of wealthy members. The majority are just hard working people who love playing the sport at a time that suits them on a golf course they enjoy. Many are also prepared to give up a lot of time, unpaid, to support the club by other means. It was therefore inevitable that these proposals would create a lot of comment from the rank and file members. There had been a lot of discussion on the subject in the weeks leading up to the meeting. Indeed such was the electricity created by this meeting that the Club Captain even went on to describe this as D-Day for the Club.

Questions were then invited from the floor. I have never been renowned for making speeches; I freely admit I am no good at them. Nevertheless I did feel strongly about the financial issues raised. The £100 debenture made sense as this was necessary to bring the general maintenance of the clubhouse up to standard but I did have reservations about the substantial mortgage planned for the proposed new building works. Plans to demolish the existing professional shop and build another on a much grander scale seemed particularly risky in a climate where the average club professional was already struggling to compete with the large golfing outlets.

It was with this in mind that I raised my hand to question the wisdom of the project and the financial burden it could put on members for years to come. The President, Jack Timms had seemed intent on avoiding my question to the point where other members finally raised a hand and suggested I be allowed to speak. Judging by the general reaction from the floor, the views of the majority of members echoed my own but to my surprise Timms' attitude towards me became rather unpleasant and offensive and this lead to calls of 'out of order' from members who considered that remarks made by him were entirely uncalled for. Concerns similar to my own followed from other members, as to the necessity of the proposed new buildings and the considerable loan needed to fund them. The EGM finally concluded and due to the ill-mannered way in which he conducted the meeting, it is probably fair to say that Jack Timms made rather a spectacle of himself that evening.

The result of the voting was basically as follows: The motion to issue £100 debentures for improvements to the clubhouse was passed, whilst the resolution for other building works, with borrowings supported by a mortgage was soundly defeated. The majority of members were clearly against taking on extensive debt, a fact borne out as members retired to the bar to discuss what had taken place. There were however exceptions to this way of thinking when later I was approached by the President. Timms had not had the best of meetings and was naturally not in the greatest of moods, so when he remarked I should not take my membership for granted, I took this as no more than an off the cuff comment from someone who was having a bad day.

Jack Timms is someone I would have regarded as an acquaintance rather than a friend. We never socialised together or played golf in the same crowd but whilst we were not close buddies, I can honestly say that in the years I had known him there was no history between us of bad feeling. We had never had any argument or dispute and other than the occurrence of the evening of the EGM, there is certainly no reason I am aware of which could justify the eventual state of affairs in which I was to find myself.

Meanwhile life continued as normal over the course of the next two months, except for the fact that I received no response at all to my correspondence regarding the land at Stubbing Lane. Although I had written in early September I had not received any reply from the Club, so by mid November I tried again. I expressed surprise that my letter had not been acknowledged. In fact I had heard nothing from the club apart from their original letter of 17th August.

I was to finally receive an acknowledgement on Christmas Eve. Apparently the matter of the land was to be discussed at the next Management Committee Meeting, due to take place on 24th January 2000. Progress of sorts would appear to be taking shape. This was the first time I had received correspondence from Hillsborough Golf Club at Christmas time, it was not to be the last.

It was during this period of non-activity by the committee that June and I had dined one evening at the club and were approached by a fellow member Garry Revitt. Garry was interested to know if there had been any recent developments regarding the sale of land. He was aware that his close friend, Philip Willers and I were both bidding for the land and seemed curious that although the bid of £75,000 made by Willers had been on the notice board for several months, my increased offer of £77,000 had not yet appeared.

I briefly relayed events (or rather lack of events) so far and voiced my own misgivings that my bid had not yet been posted, despite confirmation by Timms and two other committee members that it would be. I told Revitt that since my bid had not been put on the notice board, I had felt obliged to inform Willers myself that I had increased on his offer. Revitt then divulged that some time after the EGM in September, he had been in the company of Timms and Willers who had been having a discussion concerning the sale of the land.

Garry said it came as quite a shock when he heard Timms telling Willers **"Baker will get that land over my dead body!"** June and I were speechless. It seemed unthinkable that a club President should make such a statement, especially to the only other bidder. Aside from the personal implications involved, what right did he have to take such a decision? Timms was charged with selling off a valuable club asset. It wasn't his land after all, it belonged to the members. Surely he had a duty to act in their best interest. Non-members had already been excluded from bidding for the land and with me out of the running that left only Willers, there were no other bidders.

Naturally I asked Garry what he intended to do about it and was somewhat taken aback when he made it clear that he was not prepared to report the incident to the committee. Garry made no bones about the fact that he thought Timms' behaviour was disgraceful (in fact his exact comments were that Timms was not fit to be a member of the club, let alone President.) Nevertheless he refused to report the conversation, fearing it may also cast doubt on his friend Willers, who he felt had done nothing wrong.

Shocking as it was, Garry's disclosure did go a long way towards explaining events so far but it was of little use if he wasn't willing to confirm what he had told June and I. I pressed him on the matter but he was adamant and I certainly couldn't afford to report to the committee what Garry had said knowing he wasn't prepared to back me up. In fact in some respects I wished he hadn't said anything at all if he wasn't prepared to put his money where his mouth was so to speak.

(It perhaps should be mentioned at this point that Garry Revitt did eventually come clean regarding this revelation by Timms but this was to occur more than a year later. Revitt's belated need to unburden himself however, was not out of any desire to do the right thing, nor was it to benefit me in any way; it was a bit late in the day for that. His motive was entirely selfish but this will become apparent as the story progresses. Nevertheless a written account of that fateful conversation was in due course reported to the committee and recorded at a Management Meeting).

Meanwhile the committee met on January 24th to discuss the sale of the land. Following the meeting I received immediate correspondence, letting me know that the committee were concerned I had not accepted all of their terms and conditions and would I confirm that my offer of £78,000 was the highest I was prepared to go. This was naturally confusing since I somehow appeared to have increased my bid by £1000. Exactly when I was supposed to have done this I had no idea, nor did there seem to be any other higher bid for the land. To my knowledge Willers had not increased on his offer of £75,000. Was I bidding against myself?

Further correspondence was entered into confirming my acceptance of the terms, whilst at the same time I pointed out the committee's mistaken bid figure and requested clarification of the bidding system. I also advised that if there were higher bids I was prepared to increase on my offer.

This seemed sufficient to galvanise the committee into action but not in a way I could have foreseen.

On the 8th February 2000 I received the following letter from the President, Mr Timms:

*"Dear Mr. Baker*

   *The Club is now in a position to move on regarding the plot of land in Stubbing Lane. Unfortunately your final offer has been substantially improved upon."*

*"Thanking you for your interest"*

Who had substantially improved on the offer I had made? When had I made a final bid? I had no idea. As far as I was aware the only other bid was the £75,000 made by Mr Willers. This offer, as per club protocol, had been posted on the club notice board and it had been purely out of courtesy that I personally informed Willers I had increased on his offer. In addition of course, the knowledge of what Garry Revitt had since disclosed put a completely different light on matters.

On the 8th February 2000 maybe I should have just stopped and accepted the inevitable but then no one had had the courtesy of telling me there were higher bidders nor indeed had I made a final offer. My bid had still not been put on the club notice board, despite being told by three Officers of the Committee that all bids would be posted. I had already written expressing my confusion of the bidding system but in the vain hope that someone on the committee would see how unfairly I was being treated, I decided to give it another go. Again I wrote setting out my concerns about the bidding procedure and repeated, as in my previous letter, that I had not made a final offer but had reserved the right to do so if my bid of £77,000 had been improved upon. A reply was received as follows:

*01 March 2000*

*Dear Mr. Baker*

*"I acknowledge receipt of your letter dated 25th February 2000, which will be taken to the next Management Committee Meeting.*

*I will write to you again in due course."*

Things were now moving considerably quicker. In fact letters were now arriving at an alarming rate when only one day later I received the following:

*02 March 2000*

*Dear Mr. Baker*

*"Further to my letter of 1st March, I write to confirm that your letter of the 25th February has now been considered by the Management Committee.*

*Following a detailed and wide-ranging discussion and taking note of all the points raised by you, it was confirmed that the proposed sale of land to the other party should proceed."*

I must confess I was highly surprised that from one day to the next all members of the committee could be got together and reach a decision so quickly on a matter that was of serious financial interest to all members of the club.

None of the points I raised in my letters had been answered and I had been dismissed like a schoolmaster dismissing a child, without any courtesy or civility at all. Neither did I have any idea what bid had actually been accepted, which I would have thought that any member should be entitled to know. Maybe I was naïve but I was shocked and disgusted at what had happened. Quite apart from my personal point of view, I didn't see how the transaction had been conducted in the best interest of the membership as a whole.

That was it then! Six months of no activity and suddenly in the blink of an eye, everything had been decided regardless of any possible financial loss to the members. From what Revitt had confided it seemed perfectly obvious who was running the show and no one on the committee it seemed was prepared to question it.

My wife and I reflected on what had happened and came to the obvious conclusion that it had been decided from the offset that we would not get the land. Writing to the committee had got us absolutely nowhere and we reluctantly agreed to forget about the whole thing, take a deep breath and move on.

Over the course of the next five months very little actually happened. I continued as usual playing golf with my friends and family until early August when out of the blue I received a letter informing me *"The Management Committee of Hillsborough Golf Club requires your attendance at the next Management meeting on Monday 21st August 2000 at 7.30pm which will be held in the television room. Please confirm you are able to attend."*

Perhaps in hindsight I should have made enquiries before attending but I had never been to a committee meeting before and wasn't sure of the protocol, so at the time I merely acknowledged I would attend on the day in question. I had done nothing wrong and it never occurred to me that I was about to be hauled over the coals.

I duly arrived on the evening in question completely unaware of events which were about to unfold. Members of the committee had their agenda for the meeting and I alone was blissfully ignorant of the bombshell waiting to be dropped. The proceedings during the course of that meeting put into motion events that sadly, without trying to appear too dramatic, were to affect the course of my life as I had known it. Nevertheless at the allotted time on 21st August 2000, I entered the committee room to be faced with a full committee seated either side of a long table. The President, Jack Timms headed the table. The whole scenario rather gave off the impression of being a Spanish inquisition.

The President began the meeting by informing me that I had made remarks to another club member about building contracts being carried out at the club. It was alleged that I had accused this member and the President of being involved in some sort of price fixing. I was staggered. I immediately asked who had made the complaint. Timms refused to divulge the name but I was insistent and repeatedly pressed him on the matter. Finally Timms relented and said the complaint had been made by a fellow member Derek Brown. To say I was shocked would be a serious understatement. I had turned up at the request of the committee and completely out of the blue was being accused of a serious allegation. Naturally, since I had never made any such remarks, I totally refuted the accusation. (A fact subsequently confirmed by the minutes of the meeting.)

Why would anyone make such remarks to Derek Brown anyway, especially as he was a very close friend of Timms? Apart from anything else I didn't know of any contracts at the club involving Timms and Brown.

During the course of the meeting only the President, Jack Timms, spoke. This was a surprise in itself since there were other members of the committee seated around the table who were usually quite voluble and forthright in both their opinions and statements. In particular there was Ted Laycock, a past President, notorious for quoting not only the rules on golf but on all club matters. Very rarely did a general meeting of the club go by without him having his six pennies worth on one subject or another. Quite honestly you would have thought that he had swallowed the book on rules. He of all people must surely have realised at the time that my rights as a member were being infringed but on this particular occasion he seemed to have been gripped by a severe case of amnesia.

I was subsequently asked to leave the meeting whilst the committee considered its decision.

I must confess my mind was in turmoil. I was extremely angry but to be honest I have to admit I was also quite worried by the whole event. Having to face a panel of people like some naughty schoolboy where false allegations were being made against me was bad enough but added to this was the fact that the complaint I had allegedly made involved Jack Timms and he was also heading the investigation into the complaint. That was an experience I think that would have unnerved the best of us. To make matters worse, the remarks Timms made at the previous year's EGM, (concerning my membership) suddenly began filtering through my mind.

The committee, as I subsequently found out by requesting the relevant minutes, had agreed that I be sent a letter stating that the matter was now closed but should I at any time in the future behave in a manner which could be considered against the interests of Hillsborough

Golf Club and its members, then action would be taken. As you will see as you go through this book, the committee of Hillsborough Golf Club are good at deeming matters to be closed, particularly when it suited their own cause.

Of course at this stage I didn't know all this, I was outside the meeting room pacing the floor and waiting to be called back in by my inquisitors. This duly happened and the President asked me if I doubted the integrity of the committee or any of its members. It seemed a funny question to ask but what could I say? I had to reply I had every confidence in the committee and left it at that. It did not seem wise to give any other answer.

I was not advised at the time but it later came to light that the Club have Rules of Procedure for dealing with allegations and matters of a disciplinary nature. Most importantly the accused member must be given notification of any complaint or allegation made against them. In the event of a disciplinary hearing, the member is to be advised of this in writing and also given the opportunity to take along a fellow member to the meeting. On this particular occasion however, none of the required procedures were followed.

On the 1st September I received a letter from the President, which read as follows:

*"Further to your attendance before the committee on 22nd August 2000 and after due deliberation by the committee it was decided on this occasion to overlook your alleged actions.*

*However if the committee find their trust in you*

*has been abused they will have no alternative other
than to take the matter further.*

*We trust that there will be no need to take further
action and hope you will continue to enjoy the
benefits of being a member of Hillsborough Golf
Club."*

It was clear from the letter that it had obviously been
decided that I was guilty of the charge, despite the fact I
had told them it was completely untrue. My word
apparently was not to be believed. Sure they offered to
overlook it on this occasion but as far as I was concerned
there was nothing to overlook. I had done nothing wrong
since I had not made the allegation in the first place.
More to the point, how was I to know if and when I
would abuse their trust in the future since it seemed to be
decided by the committee on a totally ad hoc basis. The
parting shot had not instilled any confidence either.
What 'further action' could they take when I hadn't done
anything and why, I wondered had it been necessary to
mention my continued membership?

The complaint itself was ludicrous. Not to put too fine
a point on it, what member apart from a complete idiot
would be stupid enough to accuse the President of the
Club of corruption, let alone make the accusation to one
of the President's closest friends? Some members of the
committee were people I had known for a number of
years. I had played golf and snooker with them and we
got on well. I voted for some when they put up for
committee. A couple of them actually approached me a
day or so after the meeting and confided that Timms had
been completely out of order. They suggested I should

take no notice but that was easy for them to say, sitting as they were on opposite sides of the fence so to speak. I should have asked why they didn't speak up at the meeting, in fact on reflection there are probably a number of thing I should have said or done differently but that would be with the benefit of hindsight of course.

Aggrieved and disappointed by the response, I wrote back emphasising that the allegation was completely without foundation. I requested that this be recorded and that the committee acknowledge this fact.

Towards the end of September I received a reply signed by John Hall, who had joined the committee in March as Vice Captain. John is also someone I have known for over 50 years. We went to school together and his sister is married to my brother. In other words we go back an awful long way. The letter began, Dear Mr Baker and rather seemed to set the tone for the collapse of my friendship with John Hall, which I intend to detail later in this book.

The main crux of this letter (which Hall agreed to sign but later informed me that it had in fact been written by Jack Timms) is quoted below:

*"We write to confirm the true position which is that matters were raised with you by the management committee and your replies were noted.*

*In view of your assurances that you fully accepted the integrity of the management committee and each member of the committee, it was decided that no further investigation of the matters raised would be made. The committee also felt it would not be in the interest of the club to create an inquisition and hoped this matter would end there and then."*

The letter closed:

*"However if you are still not prepared to let this matter end, the member who made the allegations is fully prepared to attend the next committee meeting and repeat these allegations.*

*The committee will then after due deliberation reach a decision which will be final."*

So despite denying the charge, I still stood accused of making defamatory remarks regarding a club member and the golf club President. I couldn't believe it. How could the committee do this without any evidence to back up the allegation? It was all very well to say now 'that it was not in the club's interest to create an inquisition' but from my point of view the inquisition had already taken place and despite my denying the allegation, it had obviously been decided that I was guilty. All the same the last few lines of the letter, signed by John Hall of all people, were a clear threat to my membership if I did not let the matter drop.

I didn't know what to do. I had not made any allegation against the President, Derek Brown or anyone else for that matter. Like many other members at the club, I was well aware of the fact that Timms wielded a lot of power at Hillsborough. He evidently wanted me out, (why else would he make up such a story) and there didn't appear to be much resistance coming from the committee, apart from those who had privately confessed some sympathy but that was of little consolation if they were not willing to stand up and be counted. The rumourmongers had also been busy spreading the message that I had been a bad boy but the committee had kindly let me off with a warning. The wording of Timms' letter following the disciplinary meeting was beginning to weigh heavily on my mind. *"However if the committee find their trust in you has been abused they will have no alternative other than to take the matter further."*

I had no way of stopping the rumours, I could explain the allegation was obvious rubbish but undoubtedly this would be construed as 'abusing the committee's trust'. It was extremely frustrating. As time passed, the more it played on my mind. Thanks to Timms I now had one black mark against my name and deep down I knew if he got away with it this time, it wouldn't be the last. I thought long and hard about the options open to me.

It was my wife June who suggested the most suitable option and one I agreed to, although not without a certain degree of trepidation. She suggested I should contact Derek Brown and sort this matter out once and for all. It wasn't the first time she had made this suggestion but knowing Brown was a close friend of Timms, I was reluctant to speak to him. The point had now come where it seemed I had nothing to lose. On reflection I found it difficult to believe that Brown could have made such an incredible allegation. I certainly wouldn't describe him as a close friend, we didn't often play golf at the same times or in the same crowd but we had occasionally chatted in the bar and bought each other a pint. I had actually always quite liked the bloke. Even so, I had to assume that Timms was behind the whole thing and Brown, for whatever reason had gone along with it.

On the afternoon of 18th January 2001 I telephoned Derek Brown. We had a conversation where I outlined that I had been having a problem with the committee as a result of a complaint he had made. I didn't go into detail or make any mention of Jack Timms or his involvement. Brown's reaction was interesting to say the least. He was shocked to hear what had happened. He genuinely had no idea that I had been in front of the committee. Brown confirmed he had no reason to make any complaint about me. I pressed him on the matter but he assured me he had made no complaint, either verbal or in writing. Brown also kindly agreed that John Hall, the Vice Captain could ring and verify this. After expressing my relief, I thanked Brown for his time and immediately rang John. That same afternoon John called me back. He confirmed that Brown had repeated these same facts to him. I felt an enormous weight had been lifted from my shoulders.

As far as I could see the only person who was intent on making false accusations against me was the Club President, Jack Timms. After my initial experience with him and the committee, I had reservations about dealing with them direct and decided instead to have a chat with my Solicitor, Jeremy Peel. I told him about the false allegation and by way of background I also relayed to him the story regarding the sale of the land, although I stressed I had taken the decision to move on after the land incident and had not pursued it. It was agreed that the two events were interlinked and combined they clearly showed that Timms had some sort of grudge against me. Acting on my behalf, Mr Peel sent a letter to the Golf Club on 7th February 2001.

The letter referred to the sale of the land at Stubbing Lane, pointing out that I had not been given the opportunity to place a final bid and the land had been sold 'subject to planning consent' to Philip Willers despite the fact that I would have increased my offer. (No mention was made of Garry Revitt's revealing insight into the conversation between Timms and Willers, where it was indicated that my only chance of obtaining the land would be in the event of Timms' untimely demise.)

At this stage it was also pointed out that I did not know how much Willers had bid for the land despite the fact that such information, one would assume, should be made available to all members of the club, since they would be the ultimate beneficiaries of any sale. In short it was stated that there had not been a fair and reasonable bidding process and that the land had been sold to Willers without further enquiries being made about possible higher bids.

The letter then moved on to cover the meeting in August 2000, where the President had read out a complaint, allegedly made by fellow club member Derek Brown, that I had alleged corrupt or underhand dealings in connection with building contracts being allocated at the club. It was also pointed out that Derek Brown had never made any allegation against me, either verbally or in writing and was both astonished and shocked that I had been called before the committee to answer such an allegation when none had been made. It was further emphasised that not only had Derek Brown confirmed this to me, he had also repeated the same facts to the

Vice Captain, John Hall.

The letter continued:

*"It does not appear that there was any allegation in writing from Mr. Brown to prompt the calling of the Committee Meeting and it appears patently clear that Mr. Timms has a personal grudge against Mr. Baker for some reason best known to Mr. Timms and has used (or rather abused) his position of office as President to attempt to discredit Mr. Baker and even to put Mr. Baker's membership of the club in jeopardy.*

*In summary therefore the complaint is as follows:*

*In the handling of the sale of the land although Mr Baker's correspondence speaks for itself, his letters of 3rd February 2000 and 25th February 2000 in particular quite clearly indicate his intention to make an increased offer to counter that of another bidder should the need arise. Quite possibly therefore the land has been sold for less than might have been, possibly to the detriment of all members of the Club.*

*Mr. Baker was brought before the Committee for a Disciplinary Meeting (he firmly believes at the sole initiative of the President) in respect of an allegation that transpires never to have been made."*

We asked that this serious complaint be investigated by the committee and that we be informed of the result of the investigation as soon as possible.

This first solicitor's letter was to reveal to me the true workings of the committee at Hillsborough Golf Club and the power it held over certain members. As I was to find out, some people held firm but many did exactly as the committee said irrespective of the rights or wrongs of their actions. Derek Brown belonged firmly in the latter category.

# Chapter 2

# The Cover Up

I was still blissfully unaware of it at the time but in between my solicitor's letter being sent out and Hillsborough Golf Club replying, worms had already begun to turn. Derek Brown was approached by a member of the committee and 'suddenly decided' to change his story. Despite having assured the Vice Captain, John Hall and me that he had no reason to make any complaint about me at all, Brown was apparently paid a visit by the Captain, Bob Turnbull armed with a copy of my solicitor's letter, whereupon Brown immediately proceeded to draft a letter directly contradicting everything he had previously confirmed. It was really quite astonishing. Any unbiased committee would surely have asked Brown to explain his reasons for giving an entirely opposite account from the one he had made only four weeks earlier. In fact what motive did the Captain have in approaching Brown at all when Brown had already made his position perfectly clear to the Vice Captain?

The obvious step would have been to question Jack Timms as to why he had made a serious allegation against another member when it clearly wasn't true but then Timms was President of the Club, so the committee decided to use their discretion. Following the premise 'if you don't want the answer – don't ask the question' they evidently came to the conclusion that it was better not to ask Timms anything at all.

Whilst I didn't know Derek Brown particularly well, it was common knowledge that he was a close friend of both Timms and the Captain, Bob Turnbull and that all three were regular golfing partners. Did Timms and the committee panic when they received my solicitor's letter? Brown was obviously asked to put his letter together in response but having already confirmed the exact opposite, Brown's letter really wasn't worth the paper it was written on.

As you will see in this book, it was a long and arduous process trying to get sight of Brown's letter, in fact it was continuously withheld from both my solicitor and me despite many requests to have sight of it. If it had been truthful what possible reason could there be in refusing me permission to have a copy? In any case Brown's letter along with the initial missive from my solicitor appeared to have opened a large can of worms, a can that in my opinion is still open.

A response was received from the Golf Club on 27th February in a 'without prejudice' letter, a statement that seemed ironic bearing in mind the contents. My solicitor's letter had been discussed at a Management Meeting on 19th February. All members of the committee apparently attended with the exception of Jack Timms.

On the question of the land at Stubbing Lane it was stated *"the Committee considered at length all correspondence and relevant management meeting minutes. The Committee was unanimous in confirming that the decision reached on the sale of the land was the correct decision that satisfied the best interest of the*

*Golf Club. However the committee would confirm that although they accepted the highest offer it was not only under a duty to accept the highest financial offer but to take into account other aspects of the bids received. The Committee also confirms that at no time was it agreed or stated that all bids received for the land would be displayed on the Club notice board"*

What 'other aspects' could they be referring to? As far as I was aware at the time, no one had bid higher than me but the club was now freely admitting that it had no intention of conducting an open sale for the land amongst its bidders. It seemed they had a preferred buyer for the land and that was final. One would have thought the club would have welcomed other bids if they were to obtain the best price for the land.

The letter then went on to refer to the alleged allegation by Timms and Brown.

*"The Committee considered a letter from Mr. D Brown dated 17th February 2001 which clearly states that Mr. D Brown had received comments from your client, which suggested that Mr. D Brown and the President Mr. J Timms were involved in some sort of price fixing. Mr. D Brown was extremely annoyed by the allegations made by your client and shortly afterwards reported these comments to the President. These were the comments referred to in the disciplinary meeting with your client.*

*Following this disciplinary meeting the Committee decided that it would be in the best interests of the Club not to take the complaints against your client any further. This decision was reached, taking into account your clients statement at the meeting, that he did not doubt the integrity of the Committee or any of its members.*

*In these circumstances, the Committee expect that your client will unreservedly withdraw all allegations against the Committee and submit a written apology to the President."*

This was written by the Vice President, Bruce Oakes and signed by the Club Secretary, Thomas Pigott. Unfortunately I was destined to have many more dealings with both of these characters.

Going back to the committee's reply, apparently Derek Brown was extremely annoyed by the comments I had allegedly made. Only one month earlier he had stated quite categorically that he had not made a complaint and had no reason to make one. He was not even aware that I had been in front of a disciplinary meeting.

This letter by Brown was in effect being used by the committee as a basis for a disciplinary meeting which had taken place six months prior to the letter being written. I very much doubt the committee could have anticipated Brown would write such a letter so long after my meeting with them. It looked to me more and more like a spur of the moment 'please get us out of trouble' letter. Either way, the letter Derek Brown had now apparently written was really of no consequence, other than it may be defamatory and was evidence only of the fact that Brown had now lied. In August when I faced the committee there was no letter, there was no allegation, in short there was no reason for me to be at the meeting at all. The whole thing had been a complete sham. A figment of Timms' imagination and this letter produced six months later did nothing to change that. In fact the letter belonged exactly where any fair committee would have filed it; directly in the waste bin.

Brown's assurance to Hall (that he had no reason at all to make any complaint about me) was made clear in the letter from my solicitor but in their reply the committee simply ignored this. Neither did they give any explanation at all for Brown having suddenly changed his story following a visit to him by the Club Captain. If this was the case, then he had given two entirely opposite accounts to different Officers of the Club. They couldn't both be true. Why was this not questioned?

Under normal circumstances Brown would doubtless have been explaining himself before the committee but the events taking place here were clearly far from normal. The committee could quite easily clear up this matter once and for all by having Timms, Brown and me together at a meeting, where the truth could be established and where the Captain and Vice Captain could also give their account. The committee did not object when I had to attend a meeting even though there was no reason for me to be there.

I was annoyed and confused by the club's letter since at the time none of it made sense.

I immediately rang John Hall. He explained that just prior to the Management Meeting he had been waylaid by the Captain, Bob Turnbull. There was a brief discussion between the two where John relayed the details of his telephone conversation with Brown.

Turnbull responded that he had personally met with Derek Brown and would deal with the matter himself.

I was dumbfounded since I could hardly believe my ears. John was saying he had attended the meeting but did not report his conversation with Brown basically because Bob Turnbull told him not to and John had simply gone along with this. I didn't want to believe what I was thinking but everyone knew how close Turnbull, Timms and Brown were. I should have thought it was obvious to anyone what was happening here.

Words could not do justice to the way I felt. I had known John most of my life and trusted him implicitly. I felt sickened by what he had allowed to happen. If John had reported his conversation with Brown at that meeting, Turnbull could not have simply produced a letter from Brown stating the complete opposite without the matter being debated. I told John in no uncertain terms exactly how I felt and replaced the receiver. Shortly afterwards he rang back but I couldn't bring myself to talk to him and June took the call instead.

John asked if he could come over and speak to us. When he arrived he admitted he had made a terrible mistake and seemed genuinely upset. He explained that he had left the matter with Turnbull and the moment passed when he should have stood up and spoken out. He now regretted what had happened and was full of apologies. He made the lame excuse that there seemed little point in speaking out once Brown had written a letter saying something completely different. I on the other hand couldn't see where John's brains were, as far as I was concerned that was all the more reason to speak out there and then and I told him so.

I believe there are times when it takes just one person to stand up and be counted and I honestly feel this was one of them. If John had spoken up initially and made absolutely clear at that Management Meeting that he wasn't prepared to go along with Brown's 'miraculous memory recall' then I seriously doubt that any of the subsequent events would have taken place. My family and I would not have been made to suffer the most dreadful experience and I would not be writing this book.

When John left that day he was full of good intentions. He offered to sign an account of his conversation with Brown and planned to organise a meeting with the other committee members, where he intended to put matters right by confirming what Brown had told him. Unfortunately, John was to discover that certain members of the committee were not so keen to hear what he had to say. This in itself came as no surprise to me, when John returned the following day with the news that a special meeting could not be arranged.

It was obvious at that point that John did have a conscience; unfortunately he didn't have the strength of character to do what his conscience told him. He was at a crossroads and sadly for me he took the wrong path. John's resolve to do the right thing, however genuine at the time, turned out to be very short lived. Maybe pressure came to bear from some of the more prominent members of the committee. John was shortly to become the next Captain of the Club. Perhaps he was given the 'acting in the best interest of Hillsborough Golf Club' speech which roughly translated means, when one of our own is in trouble we all close ranks. This way of thinking, as he was later to discover, turned out to be of crucial benefit to John himself further along in this story.

The very next response I was to receive on behalf of the golf club committee was to arrive within a week of John taking over his role as Captain of the Club. This new Captain of Hillsborough turned out to be a very different person from the John I had grown up with and considered to be a close friend for the past fifty years. This in itself was probably one of the hardest things to accept in all that subsequently happened to me and to my wife and son.

Meanwhile my solicitor replied. He raised the point that just ten days after our letter of complaint, someone had asked Mr Brown to write a letter in which Mr Brown had now apparently made in writing the complaint that was raised at the Disciplinary Meeting last August. My solicitor requested sight of Brown's letter.

Peel wrote *"Since receiving your letter Mr. Baker has spoken to the current Vice Captain, John Hall who has stated that he did confirm to Mr. Turnbull what Derek Brown had said but that he did not say anything in committee when perhaps with hindsight he should have done. It seems that Mr. Hall was never invited by the committee during either of the committee meetings to state whether or not what was stated in our letter was correct"*

Peel went on to say: *"we find this absolutely astonishing. It would have been the obvious thing for the Committee to ask Mr. Hall what had been said or had not been said by Mr. Brown and for this to be minuted.*

*Our client is quite confident that if he had been asked directly, Mr. Hall would have confirmed the truth, which is as per our letter. We respectfully suggest that the Committee reconsiders and asks Mr. Hall in a Committee Meeting directly since our client is quite sure that Mr. Hall will be entirely truthful when asked directly."*

Regarding the land at Stubbing Lane my solicitor replied *"In various letters our client made reference to the procedure whereby bids were to be placed on the member's notice board. In particular we refer to the letters written by our client to the Secretary dated 3rd February 2000 and 25th February 2000. At no stage did anybody seek to point out that our client's letters were wrong in stating that bids would be displayed on the notice board. Why was this not pointed out if the matter is as stated in your letter?"*

Clarification was also requested of what other aspects could possibly be involved in the sale of the land. *"We cannot think therefore what these "other aspects" could possibly be and would invite you to make this clear. Even if there were relevant "other aspects" these factors should have been made clear to both interested bidders."*

Needless to say this was not made clear; in fact 'other aspects' were never again mentioned in any correspondence, either from the club or their solicitor.

Peel continued *"The fact remains that the Club has failed to obtain the best price for the land and your letter does not make clear why the Committee did not accept the highest financial offer that may have been made (namely if our client had been given a fair and reasonable opportunity to improve on the offer made by the other bidder.) Had our client been informed of the other bidder's offer (whether by display on the Club Notice Board or in some other way) our client would have improved his offer but for obvious reasons he was not prepared to bid against himself as his correspondence made clear."*

In conclusion *"We feel sure that in these circumstances any independent person reading this correspondence would readily understand why these matters have been raised and why it is felt that there has not been a proper explanation or investigation of our client's complaint. We ask that this be remedied as quickly as possible."*

Well we certainly felt that we deserved a proper explanation but the committee thought differently. They had demanded that I withdraw my complaint and make an apology to the President, a written one at that. No doubt that instruction came from Timms himself. I can well imagine the amount of coverage he would have made of that scenario. It would have seen more circulation than the club news letter. What had I done that warranted an apology to Timms? Any apologies should be directed from Timms to me not the other way around. His bigoted comments to Willers were explicit enough; he intended to make sure I would not get the land and he succeeded. Not content with this, he decided to haul me in front of the committee and make a false allegation against me. The man was prejudiced, how much evidence did they need?

The committee however took the decision to sidestep the whole issue and bring in the cavalry instead.

So it was at this stage that the Committee of Hillsborough Golf Club decided to instruct a firm of solicitors. The President's conduct had been inexcusable. He had taken advantage of his position and his actions had clearly put my membership at risk. I was fully entitled to request that the committee investigate; they and only they had the authority to conduct an enquiry and take action on any wrongdoing. Why did the committee or indeed Timms need legal representation if everything that had been done was above board and there was nothing to hide? If this was the case why not simply deal with my enquiry instead of running up legal fees for members?

It was on April 5th 2001 that the Club's solicitor wrote the first of many letters with the heading,

*"Re; Our Client; Hillsborough Golf Club Limited*
*Your Client; Roger Baker"*

The crux of their first letter contained the following points:

*"The Club did not decide to offer the land for sale by a system of open bidding with bids being placed on the Members Notice Board."*

Now this seemed clear enough but if this was so, why did the committee not clarify this issue whilst the land was being sold? I had written them letters pointing out my confusion on this very point. They could have simply replied that I was mistaken and explained what the bidding system was. If the club wanted the best price for the land surely that would have been the obvious thing to do.

*"We note that Mr Baker has instructed you that he was assured by various Officers of the Club that each bid would be placed on the notice board. As this was not the system the Committee finds this allegation extraordinary. Will your Client provide the names of the Officers concerned, the dates of the conversations and details of what was said".*

I had not made an allegation, what I had said was quite simply a statement of fact. It seemed to me the committee had a great deal of trouble in distinguishing the difference between these two things. Perhaps the committee would not find this so extraordinary when I subsequently provided them, not only with the names of the Officers concerned but also their written confirmation of these conversations.

Speaking of extraordinary allegations, none could be more so than the one Timms claimed had been made by Brown, especially as Brown later denied making it. The committee's insistence on pursuing this allegation instead of withdrawing it was all the more extraordinary; nevertheless no-one seemed to have the slightest problem with this.

*"The proposals as to sale were set out in writing to your client and to Mr. Willers in a letter dated 17th August 1999. The Committee were entitled to draw the bidding process to a close by giving your client a final deadline to make his best offer which they did. The Committee were entitled to proceed on the basis they set out when met with a letter seeking to impose conditions. Your client was well aware that he had*

*seven days from 25th January 2000 to make any increase on his offer of £77,000"*

This was not strictly accurate. The committee had asked if £78,000 was in fact my highest and final offer. Allowing for the fact that £78,000 was not the amount I had bid, I replied advising them of this error, whilst at the same time I expressed my confusion of the bidding process. I also clearly stated that I wished to reserve the right to make a higher offer if my previous bid of £77,000 had been increased upon, there being little point in doing so otherwise, surely this was clear enough.

*"We are instructed that the Committee Meeting your client was asked to attend was a Management Meeting not a disciplinary meeting"*

This was the most amazing claim yet and quite frankly it was also an insult to anyone's intelligence.

Of course it was a Disciplinary Meeting! The Vice President, Mr Bruce Oakes should refer to his own letter written just a few weeks earlier. Under the section headed <u>ALLEGATIONS,</u> written in capital letters and underlined, he would find not once but three times he referred to the meeting I had attended as a Disciplinary Meeting. A full committee was gathered around the table whilst the President, Jack Timms proceeded (without any prior warning) to make a completely untrue allegation against me and the meeting was subsequently confirmed to me as a Disciplinary Meeting. I was certainly not invited to the meeting to offer up an opinion on course management or to discuss the condition of the greens.

It was patently obvious why the committee now chose to make this claim. The meeting had contravened all Disciplinary Procedures. The committee did not inform me that it was to be a Disciplinary Meeting, or indeed that an allegation had been made, let alone the nature of the allegation. Neither was I informed that I was entitled to take along a fellow member for support and who, more importantly in this instance, could have borne witness to this pantomime. In addition, the committee saw no conflict of interest in the fact that the 'alleged complaint', not only involved Timms but he was also conducting the investigation. I suppose in the interest of fairness and impartiality, this meant that once I had denied the allegation, Timms would then go on to question himself and Mr Brown?

*"We can confirm that the comments made by Mr. Brown to the President were verbal and were not confirmed in writing prior to the Management Meeting. Mr Brown has now in connection with your letter of 7th February confirmed in writing his recollection of the comments made by your client. In fairness to Mr Brown he did not make a formal complaint to the Committee and that is why the Meeting was not a disciplinary hearing. However comments had been made and the Committee decided these were considered serious and should not be ignored"*

I apologise if we seem to be going around in circles a little here but again we appear to be looking at comments that Derek Brown never made until asked by the Captain, Mr Turnbull to put a letter together on the 17th February, a letter which as already stated (and forgive me for repeating this) is the exact opposite of what he had confirmed to John Hall and myself just four weeks earlier.

*"We are instructed by the Committee to request you to confirm that your client accepts that the Committee has always acted with probity and good faith.*

*If your client is not prepared to confirm this the Committee will consider whether his continuing conduct is injurious to the Club pursuant to Article 16 of the Articles of Association."*

Well that was it, written on the instructions of the committee and paid for by Club Members. It seemed whatever the committee said you had to agree with, whether it was true or not was completely irrelevant. Their word was law. It was not my conduct that was in question here; nevertheless I was being threatened with expulsion. The final paragraph of the letter was clear enough - agree with us or you're out!

So I was to confirm under threat of expulsion (i.e. Article 16) that the committee had always acted with 'probity and good faith'. I checked the exact definition of the word probity just to be sure. It means honesty, integrity and honour. Nothing the committee had done so far in connection with this whole affair had displayed any of those qualities and I'd be damned before I would be willing to confirm that they had. The committee would just have to go ahead and expel me, although what possible grounds they had for kicking me out, I had no idea. One thing was sure; they were certainly going to do everything in their power to find one.

The committee had already demanded that I withdraw all allegations and submit a written apology to the President. It seemed they were quite prepared to go along with the false allegation Timms had made and the cover up by his mate Brown and what was more incredible, they were threatening to expel me because I wasn't willing to go along with it as well.

If you had asked me then what Article 16 of the Association actually said, I could quite honestly say I did not have a clue. Now two and a half years later I know every word, every comma and every full stop off by heart. So does my wife June and my son Ricky. I also know, as you will see later in this tale, that it only applies to certain people and rarely, if ever to HGC committee members, regardless of their actions. Actually this is hardly surprising when bearing in mind the wording of the first line of Article 16, *"If any member shall in the opinion of the Committee"*... If the justification for expelling a member rests on the opinion of the committee then I for one didn't stand a chance. I have taken the liberty of quoting the Article here in full.

*"If any member shall in the opinion of the Committee be guilty of any conduct injurious to the Club, such a Member shall be liable to expulsion by a resolution of the Committee. Provided that notice of the meeting of the Committee at which such resolution is intended to be submitted and of the intended resolution shall be given to such Member, who shall also have an opportunity of giving orally or in writing at such Meeting, and before the*

*intended resolution is submitted, any explanation or defence he or she may think fit."*

I realise it sounds a bit of a mouthful but in plain English it simply means the all powerful committee are judge and jury and whatever they say goes.

Regardless of the threat to my membership, the prospect of writing a grovelling apology to Timms was simply unthinkable. From where I stood if I gave in now my days in the club were numbered anyway. Quite frankly I felt I had no choice but to continue. I was not guilty of the allegation made; there was clear evidence of this and I needed to clear my name.

The next month was devoted to going around in circles, particularly where trying to get access to Derek Brown's letter was concerned. Despite the fact that the letter made allegations against me, it was apparently to be hidden away for consumption by Brown and the Committee Members of Hillsborough Golf Club only.

On 11<sup>th</sup> May my solicitor made yet another attempt to have sight of the letter:

*"As regards the letter from Mr. Brown surely this letter is the property of the Golf Club and its members and is not Mr. Brown's property. We are therefore at something of a loss to understand why Mr. Brown's permission is needed before the letter is released. This letter was requested by us as long ago as 1st March of this year and this is now over 10 weeks ago. It appears that this letter makes allegations against our client, which are certainly denied and which may even be defamatory and our*

*client must be entitled to a copy of that letter and we reiterate that we do not understand why Mr. Brown's permission is required before the letter is released. Could we please hear from you with a copy of the letter as quickly as possible?"*

The reply was very short and to the point:

*"Your client has no entitlement to see this letter. Our client is quite entitled to take what steps it feels appropriate."* Well that was clear enough.

I was the one who had had defamatory remarks made against me yet according to the committee I apparently was the one with no rights. Presumably this meant that the committee was perfectly happy for anyone to go around making defamatory remarks about a member, providing if when it suited them they could then just sweep them under the carpet.

If the allegation was true what did the committee or Derek Brown have to hide?

One possible answer to this was the statement signed by Vice Captain, John Hall and dated 3rd March 2001.

*"I wish to make clear the details as told to me by Derek Brown in January 2001. Derek Brown confirmed to me that he had never made any written or verbal complaints against Roger Baker and he had no reason whatever to do so."*

This was written in connection with the conversation Hall had with Brown, straight after my own conversation with him on 18th January and clearly contradicted

44

Brown's letter of 17th February where he 'suddenly recalled' myself making an allegation.

By 23rd May, my solicitor Mr Peel was himself becoming increasingly frustrated at the way the committee were conducting themselves and took the most unusual step of writing a letter completely off his own bat as it were, in which he expressed his personal views in crystal clear fashion. I appreciate the gesture made by Mr Peel on my behalf and I have taken the liberty of quoting the main points of his letter:

*"We would have thought that any Organisation or Club that considered itself to be run on even remotely equitable and fair procedures would fully accept that a member against whom an allegation has been made is entitled to a sight of a copy of any document setting out that allegation. We are surprised that your clients do not appreciate and agree with this. It is our view (and we are speaking now of our view as Solicitors and not the view of our client) that it is called into question what either Mr. Brown or the Committee or both have to hide. It seems to us that there can be no other explanation."*

*"If Mr. Brown had no reason to make a complaint about Mr. Baker as at January 2001 there is no explanation for him having committed to writing any complaint. Mr. Baker is entitled on the basis of any definition of the Rules of Natural Justice to a sight of the letter making this complaint."*

A copy of Mr Hall's statement of 3rd March was enclosed with Peel's letter.

This seemed to change the club's tactics and on 25th May the Club's solicitor now wrote the following:

*"Our clients have not refused to disclose a copy of the letter in question to you. They are simply as a matter of courtesy seeking Mr. Brown's permission first."* Well at least this was an improvement on *"Your client has no entitlement to see this letter"*

The letter was the property of the Club and the committee had now had three months in which to produce it. If Mr Brown's permission was being asked as stated (simply as a matter of courtesy) and he had not given it, then surely the Club had been courteous enough and should do the right thing and release the letter anyway.

So we moved on with still no sign of the offending letter. Three other letters were written however, which on the face of it should have strengthened my case considerably.

I had approached the officers of the club who had previously assured me that all bids were to be posted on the notice board and they confirmed in writing what they had said. The third person had been Timms himself but I wasn't about to speak to him on any subject.

The first letter from Henry Barber, at that time Handicap Secretary, kindly confirmed the following: I use the word 'kindly' here because it seemed a nice thing to do at the time. As you will see later I would have a different choice of words these days.

*"Following a request from Roger Baker I did make enquiries with Jack Timms as to whether Mr Baker's*

bid of £77,000 would be placed on the member notice board. Jack Timms confirmed that all bids would be posted and I then conveyed this information to Mr Baker."

This was good of Barber since it showed that the bidding procedure the club should have followed was not implemented, well certainly not as far as my bid was concerned. It also made a complete nonsense of the committee's claim that *"as this was not the system the Committee finds this allegation extraordinary"*

Bob Turnbull also wrote:
*"I can confirm that during my term of office as Vice Captain of Hillsborough Golf Club Mr Roger Baker approached myself and asked if his offer for the land off Stubbing Lane would go on the Notice Board. I made enquiries and contacted Mr Baker to inform him that his offer would be posted on the Notice Board".*

Even more positive from my viewpoint was a letter from John Hall (now Captain of the Club) which included the following statement by Garry Revitt:

*"Conversation between Mr. J. Timms and Mr. P. Willers and witnessed by Mr. G Revitt when Jack Timms stated that you (Roger Baker) " would get the land over his dead body".*

This conversation was reported in a Committee Meeting by Hall and was minuted at that meeting.
Earlier in the story you may recall that whilst bidding was in progress for the land at Stubbing Lane, Garry

Revitt had confided to June and I about the conversation he had witnessed between Timms and Willers. Revitt had refused at that time to report the matter to the committee, his concern being that this serious disclosure may also cast doubt on his friend Willers.

By March 2001 however, Revitt was about to join the ranks of the committee himself. John Hall and Revitt were good friends, regularly going on holiday together to John's apartment in Spain. John had naturally been keen that his friend should follow him as his Vice-Captain. Revitt evidently did not want any skeletons jumping out of the cupboard at an inopportune moment and finally decided it was time to put on record the conversation he had witnessed; his previous concerns about the reputation of friend Willers now seemingly forgotten. So at last it was reported and minuted, not by me a mere also-ran but courtesy of the latest recruit to the illustrious hierarchy of the Club.

It was finally official. *"Baker will get the land over my dead body,"* the assurance made by the President to the only other bidder, concerning the sale of a valuable club asset. If I had any illusions at all that the committee would be as shocked as I was on discovering this information, then I was to be sorely disappointed. The revelation, which Revitt had been reluctant to make public for so long, made no impact at all on the committee and Revitt's former opinion that Timms was not fit to be a member of the club, let alone President, no longer seemed to bother him either.

Again I turned to my solicitor for help the upshot being that a detailed letter setting out all events to date was sent on the 2nd July. Yet again we asked for release of Brown's letter. The committee had still refused to clear my name of the allegation which had now been going on for nearly a year and it was causing a great deal of stress to me and my family. In an attempt to put a stop to all this I instructed my solicitor to suggest the following:

I would agree to attend a full Committee Meeting where all matters could be brought into the open whilst asking the committee to immediately consider the following:

To forward a copy of Brown's letter.

To cease threatening me over my continued membership of the club.

Taking into account supporting written statements from Garry Revitt, John Hall, Henry Barber and Bob Turnbull they should establish the whole truth of the background to this dispute, including questioning both Brown and Timms. I was looking forward to getting the chance to clear my name and finally putting this matter to rest. Needless to say my newfound optimism did not last. The response from the golf club was absolutely nothing.

Our letter seemed to have thrown a spanner in the works. The committee were experts when it came to avoiding awkward questions in correspondence but a meeting where everything could be brought out into the open and people questioned directly would be a different matter. It seemed inconceivable that despite the wealth of evidence now officially logged and minuted that Timms still managed to evade any enquiry into his actions.

They had accepted a conflicting statement, which the then Club Captain, Bob Turnbull had obtained from Brown and which I was still not permitted to see. They refused to question Brown about his motive in making contrasting statements and had accepted without question the scandalous comments made by Timms to Willers regarding the sale of land. They also persistently pursued a false allegation against me despite the evidence to refute it. To justify all this would be quite a task, even for the committee. A considerable amount of club funds had already been squandered on legal fees in defending Timms, when in fact his behaviour was indefensible. To alter their stance now would in all likelihood have made their own position untenable. No wonder it was taking such a long time to reply.

Whilst we received no response at all to our suggestion of a meeting, what did happen was that on July 17th 2001, John Hall came to visit me on behalf of the committee, social visits by now being a thing of the past. It was almost one year on from the Disciplinary Meeting where the allegation had first been made and apparently, or so John informed me, the allegation I had allegedly made to Derek Brown had been witnessed by another member of the club, Derek Pinning. John is the same lifelong friend who a few months previous had written confirming that Brown had never made any allegations against me at all. John followed this up by suggesting that if I were to drop my complaint against Jack Timms, the committee would be willing to delete from the company minutes and subsequent correspondence, all reference to my appearance before the Management

Committee.

June and I were stunned. The minutes are surely an important record of the Club, not something that could be tampered with when it suits the committee's purpose. If this was not a direct breach of club rules, then it must certainly be unethical at the very least. I refused point blank. I had done nothing wrong yet I was being asked by someone I had known practically all my life to get rid of the evidence that proved my innocence and (more to the point as far as I was concerned) proved Timms' guilt. John must have realised this when he made the proposition that he did. With all the evidence destroyed, how long would it be I wondered before I was accused of breaching some other regulation of the Club?

Anyway I told John exactly what my opinion of this suggestion was. John claimed he was only trying to help. Both June and I told him the only way he could help us would be to tell the truth instead of going along with the cover up for Timms. Despite our lifelong friendship, I had never realised until now what a weak man John was. I saw him in a completely new light and I didn't like what I saw. Up until this point I firmly believed that in time John would make a stand and do the right thing. Friendships were cracking and it was a crack that would eventually grow into an irretrievable chasm.

I'm quite sure John had been thrilled to be made Captain of Hillsborough Golf Club. Presumably he didn't want to rock the boat or else he needed to be seen to be doing the right things in the eyes of the committee. Whatever his reasons, all respect I ever had for him was gone and the upshot was we now had to drag Derek Pinning into the kaleidoscope of events.

Following Hall's disclosure, my solicitor had no choice but to send a letter to Pinning. He informed him of the details of the allegation that had been made by Derek Brown and that it was alleged that Pinning had witnessed this allegation. To his credit Pinning replied almost immediately on receiving the letter with a forthright denial I have quoted below:-

*"I am appalled that my name has been used by Mr. Brown as having witnessed remarks which he claims were made to him by Mr. Baker, namely that Mr. Baker accused Mr. Brown and Mr. Timms of being involved in some form of price fixing regarding a building contract at Hillsborough Golf Club.*

*I confirm that I have never witnessed such a conversation or heard Mr. Baker make any accusation of wrongdoing against Mr. Brown or Mr. Timms whatsoever"*

Peel's letter to Pinning and Pinning's reply were then fired off to the Club's solicitor.

Derek Pinning is clearly made of sterner stuff than Brown and Hall. For many years Pinning had played golf several times a week in the company of a crowd which included Jack Timms, Derek Brown and Bob Turnbull. Having been dragged into this mire so to speak, he has read all the correspondence relating to the dispute and his opinion of those involved is better left unprinted. His relationship with these former friends and golfing partners has since deteriorated to the extent that Pinning no longer associates or plays golf with them. Regardless of any personal issues involved, Derek Pinning has continued to give me his full support.

It had now been over a month since my own solicitor had sent the letter offering to meet with a full Management Committee. Despite the rising legal costs to the members it was obvious they were not keen to have a meeting, where the likes of Timms and Brown and indeed myself could be questioned, not to mention Hall, Revitt, Barber, Turnbull and now Pinning in order to finally get at the truth and put the matter to rest once and for all. As yet no reply had been forthcoming and I was still no closer to receiving a copy of Brown's letter either.

It was obvious the complaint made by Timms at the disciplinary meeting was not true. All the evidence bears this out but the committee could not acknowledge this fact and retract the allegation without exposing Brown's letter (which they had already gone along with) as a cover up. It certainly explained why John Hall had been sent as the messenger boy offering to wipe the slate clean. Despite the committee's former willingness to have me before a Disciplinary Board with no evidence at all to support the complaint, the prospect of holding a similar enquiry (with substantial proof) into the wrongdoings of Jack Timms was proving to be a different kettle of fish entirely.

The committee had a dilemma and it seemed to be taking them quite a while to decide the best way of dealing with it. Meanwhile I reflected on all that had happened since August 2000 when I had first been plunged into this endless nightmare. A year of my life had passed, though to my family and me it seemed more like ten and the committee had continued to ignore every piece of evidence put before them and unlike Timms of course, my costs were being funded from my own pocket.

By the middle of August the committee, or whoever was in the planning department, had hatched up a scheme.

The response to our request for a meeting with the full committee was that I could face an unelected tribunal to air my 'grievances'. They also specified that at such a meeting, lawyers should not be in attendance nor should witnesses be called. (Very convenient for Timms, Brown and everyone else involved.) That left just me under the spotlight once again. The reasoning behind this they claimed was that they did not want _"the forum to be elevated to the status of a judicial or quasi-judicial hearing."_ Someone had obviously spent the last month or two delving into the law books to find a way of getting everybody off the hook. Anyway back out with the dictionary for me. At least I was getting an education, I had never had occasion to look up so many big words, unfortunately this latest offering was way beyond me; I just didn't understand it.

The committee by now knew backwards what my so called 'grievances' were but it didn't matter how much proof was put under their noses, they simply would not deal with them. This was the same committee that had instigated the whole situation by indulging Timms and allowing him to make a trumped up allegation against me in the first place.

The suggested meeting was to be chaired by Michael Shaw, at that time Secretary Elect. of the National Golf Clubs' Advisory Association. Mr Shaw is also a qualified solicitor.

I had a bad feeling about this. I didn't at all fancy a meeting with a solicitor, especially as my own was not to be permitted to attend. Nothing in my view could be achieved by a meeting with an unelected tribunal that had no powers within the club to take any action at all. Anything I could possibly have to say had already been put in writing to the committee and was backed up with written evidence. Any further clarification could only come from those who had not been required to explain anything at all. Timms and Brown would obviously be a good start.

I instructed my solicitor to write back and try to get it through their heads that my 'grievance' as they put it was not with the club as such but with Timms and Brown. My concern with the club was that the committee was not willing to either perform its duty and investigate the serious allegation made against me or withdraw it. They had also refused to investigate the bidding procedure for the land it had proposed to sell. In other words the committee should consider everything on a fair and equal basis. I was merely asking that this be put into practice. It was pointed out that it had been six months since we first requested them to investigate my complaint.

Peel's letter sent at the end of August closed with the following:-

*"The only way to conclude it however is for the*

*Committee to carry out its functions properly, promptly and impartially.*

*If the Committee continues to fail to do this our client would have to consider such alternative steps as may be open to him in order to ensure firstly that Mr. Brown's letter is disclosed and secondly that some proper conclusion is reached regarding the allegations against our client that have been made by Mr. Brown and for a resolution of the allegations that our client is making (with substantial corroboration) against Mr. Timms"*

The committee remained mysteriously silent and on September 24th we tried again in terms that could not be ignored.

*"We refer to our previous correspondence and can confirm that our client has now come to the conclusion that no progress is being made nor is any progress going to be made in terms of the necessary action by the Committee. Accordingly, we are submitting the papers to Counsel so that Counsel can advise our client generally regarding both possible action against Derek Brown and our client's options as far as the Golf Club itself is concerned.*

*This action is taken with regret as far as the Golf Club is concerned but our client really is left with no alternative given that the Committee (by its inactivity) has evinced a clear intention to take no action whatsoever in respect of the matters complained notwithstanding the clearest possible evidence that has been provided"*

It took under 24 hours to get a response this time but not the response we wanted.

I was given no other option than to meet with three ex-Presidents and the Secretary of the National Golf Clubs Advisory Association. As this tribunal was unofficial and not empowered to take any disciplinary action (unlike the Committee's own Meetings) the President, Captain and Secretary obviously decided it was a meeting in which they could safely participate. The punch line of their letter was that if I refused to accept this 'reasonable suggestion' my continuing membership would apparently be brought into question. Nothing new there then! That was it. The alternative was to consider my future membership since the letter went on to accuse me of *"generally upsetting and interfering with the atmosphere of the golf club."*

My solicitor replied. He pointed out that John Hall's proposition on visiting my home was clear indication of the committee's reluctance to do anything about the matter apart from cover it up. His letter concluded *"It appears from your letter that you are saying that the Management Committee will not deal with the matter any further except of course (as suggested in the last paragraph of your letter) to threaten our client's continuing membership. It is hard to conceive of any clearer example of a Management Committee abrogating its functions."*

At around that same time Derek Pinning again wrote to the golf club. He asked why the committee had not contacted him regarding the claim that he had witnessed the alleged conversation between Derek Brown and me.

He reiterated the fact that he had not heard any such conversation and asked if it was possible to see a copy of Derek Brown's letter. Although Pinning had written previously to the committee on this issue, no-one had the courtesy to answer his letter. As you will see later in this narrative Pinning is still awaiting a reply.

I received a further letter on behalf of the Management Committee giving three alternative dates in November for the meeting with Shaw and if I didn't accept they would consider the matter closed. The parting shot, presumably on the off chance that we may have missed it in previous letters, was a final mention of 'Article 16.' I was not given any other way forward and against my better instincts, I agreed to meet with this tribunal on November 6th. I requested the names of the three ex-Presidents, although why they were attending at all seemed pointless, when only the elected Management Committee had responsibility over the question of discipline. As my solicitor was not permitted to attend, I was to be accompanied by two other club members.

It was suggested that all documentation be included for everyone to refer to at the meeting. We emphasised that once my complaints had been clarified the Management Committee should subsequently be expected to deal with the complaint and make a ruling.

Well that's what we requested. The meeting turned out slightly different.

# Chapter 3

# The Smoke Screen

So it was on the evening of November 6th 2001 that I arrived at the club to meet with the Secretary of the National Golf Clubs' Advisory Association. The function of the NGCAA is basically to protect the interests of those golf clubs that are contributing members of their Association and to assist them in the management of their affairs.

Michael Shaw, the Secretary of the Association, had just recently been appointed having assumed the post in September 2001 on the retirement of Mrs Jean Brock. Ironically enough my wife June had on one occasion played a round of golf with Jean Brock during an Invitation Day at another Sheffield Golf Club and found her to be very friendly and extremely pleasant company.

Mr Shaw is a qualified Solicitor as well as being a former Captain and President of a golf club himself. He apparently is keen to continue maintaining the close relationships which Mrs Brock developed on behalf of the Association. As you will see by the end of this meeting, I for one was not especially keen to forge a particularly close association with him.

Apart from Michael Shaw and myself, those present at the meeting were Martin Wilkes and Alf Wragg, both of whom had offered me their support. Martin is not a person to stand on the sidelines, especially when he believes there has been an injustice. Having approached me when he first heard of my problems with the club, he became involved and has been tireless in his support ever since. Alf Wragg, a highly respected member of the club for 35 years was also supportive of my stance. Sadly, Alf has since passed away and I would like to pay tribute here to Alf and his family and thank him for all his kind words and supportive actions. The three Past Presidents of the club were Joe Purseglove, an ex-policeman who I did not know particularly well, Tony Lifford an insurance agent now retired and Oliver Duffy. Also present was the current President, Bruce Oakes and Honorary Secretary Thomas Pigott as well as the Club Captain my old friend John Hall.

My own solicitor had been refused permission to attend the meeting but Mr Shaw had assured him that I would not be cross-examined. Shaw gave an undertaking that he was present to chair the meeting in his role as Secretary of the NGCAA and would look after my interests as much as those of the golf club. He went on to say that he was chairing the meeting at my request.

Why Shaw said this I had no idea. Prior to this meeting being arranged I had not previously heard of Mr Shaw or his Association and I had certainly not requested the meeting. Quite the contrary, my correspondence made clear that I wished to attend a meeting with the full Management Committee. They were elected by the members to run the club's affairs. They and only they, had authority to deal with disciplinary issues but the committee had consistently refused to hold an enquiry to investigate my complaint. How ironic that three senior members of the Management Committee had no qualms about taking part in this tribunal, which had no such powers to either make decisions or act on them and could only make procedural recommendations.

To summarise the facts;  During his term as President, Jack Timms brought a serious  allegation against me at a Disciplinary Meeting; The committee had since been provided with the clearest possible evidence that the allegation was untrue and I requested that an enquiry be held to clear my name. The only people officially empowered to do this were the elected committee, the same committee that had allowed the allegation to be made in the first place. I felt it was their duty to investigate and if the allegation proved to be unfounded, (which I knew it was) then they should withdraw it. The facts spoke for themselves and I was sure that if the club committee had been willing to conduct an impartial enquiry, the truth could quite easily have been established.

Several months earlier, Timms had already shown his true colours in his handling of the proposed sale of land. His assurance to the only other bidder that *"Baker will get the land over my dead body"* was clear indication of his intention to keep me out of the bidding and that is precisely what happened. The committee also held written evidence of this conversation.

I had been put in the wrong and was then portrayed as a troublemaker for trying to defend myself. I wanted to clear my name and set the record straight but it seemed this was construed as causing disharmony in the club, a phrase which seemed to pop up in the committee's letters with alarming regularity.

This tribunal had no authority in the club to act on any wrongdoing so from my point of view the meeting was pointless. It was just an attempt by the committee to give the impression that it was dealing with the issues, when in truth it was just a smoke screen. Something the committee could put some spin on and pass off to members as having done their best. The committee had suggested this meeting and I was confident of one thing; it was not my best interest they were thinking of. Nevertheless I had been issued an ultimatum and I have quoted below an extract from the letter concerned:

*"The Management Committee will give your client until close of business on 31st October in which to choose a day in which to air his grievances. If no date is provided The Management Committee will consider the matter closed. We are instructed that if your client does not take up this offer the view of the Management Committee is that your client has no genuine intention of airing his grievances and is only intent on generally upsetting and interfering with the atmosphere of the Golf Club.*

*Any further correspondence, other than relating to the exercise of any rights your client may have under company legislation, will be treated as a breach of Article 16 and be dealt with as such."*

Despite any impression Shaw may have been given, I hardly think anyone reading the above would consider this meeting was at my request.

Virtually from the outset I had a terrible feeling of unease about the tone of the meeting and I could sense from their reaction that Alf and Martin felt the same. We requested a short break to discuss the matter. It was obvious we all had the same misgivings. The last time I felt this way was August 2000 when I first entered the committee room that started off this dreadful chain of events.

Even at this early stage our initial instinct was to abandon the meeting but as Martin rightly pointed out, the committee would no doubt turn this to their own advantage by making it known they had done their best but Baker had walked out of the hearing and we all knew he was right; so with a certain amount of trepidation back we went.

Martin Wilkes outlined the basis of the dispute on my behalf, pointing out that Shaw had copies of the letters sent by Bob Turnbull, John Hall, Derek Pinning and others. Wilkes made particular emphasis to the letter by John Hall, confirming that Derek Brown had stated that he had no reason to make any complaint about me at all. He also reminded those present that I had still not been allowed a copy of the letter written by Derek Brown. (This was the letter promptly drafted by Brown in response to my complaint of Jack Timms and which allegedly stated the complete opposite of what he had previously confirmed.)

I was hoping after Martin Wilkes had outlined this part of my case that perhaps Shaw might ask why Brown and Timms had not been called before the committee to explain their actions. It seemed to me a natural thing to ask.

Not a bit of it! Mr Shaw, as I was to discover during the course of the meeting, was a very smooth talker on subjects he wanted to talk about and he immediately launched into a long discussion as to why neither myself nor my solicitor should be allowed sight of Brown's letter. He went on to state that the letter was between an individual member and the committee and I could not expect to receive a copy. Shaw stated he saw no problem with this and went on to express his surprise that my solicitor had requested to see it.

So having been both potentially slandered and libelled, I apparently had no right to see the letter that proves the matter one way or the other. I put this to Shaw only to be told *"it depends, certain correspondence is best not shown to other people."* But I wasn't other people, I was the victim of the complaint! Shaw went on to state that this kind of thing happens in business, in employment issues and is a matter of discretion. If there was a disciplinary meeting or action taken then apparently a person would have the right to see a copy of the letter. But I had already attended a disciplinary meeting over a year previously, a meeting where no letter of complaint had actually existed and Derek Brown, (who according to Timms had made the allegation) subsequently confirmed to both me and John Hall that he had not made any complaint about me at all.

Mr Shaw said there were clearly defects in the way the meeting had been called but since no action had been taken, then no harm had been done and it didn't matter.

No harm had been done? It didn't seem to matter to anyone that the serious charge Timms made was completely untrue. I had already spent considerable time and money trying to clear my name of a complaint which the committee would not withdraw. I had tried to ascertain why I had not been informed that it was to be a disciplinary meeting, nor had I been given any reason why I was supposed to attend. Most importantly of all I was trying to get hold of a copy of a letter, written by Brown months after the meeting, which apparently libelled me and which the committee seemed happy to take at face value, even though they had written evidence that the letter was not true.

I had done nothing wrong and yet obstacles had been continuously put in my way to prevent me from finding out the real motives of Jack Timms and Derek Brown. In addition the club committee, who would not investigate, had made several threats to my membership and demanded a written apology and I was being told that no harm had been done. The committee had willingly pursued an unfounded complaint against me but refused to conduct any enquiry into Timms, despite the substantial written evidence to support such an enquiry.

I had already emphatically told the committee that I had made no allegation against Timms and Brown, a fact initially backed up by Derek Brown himself and although there was not a shred of proof to the allegation, the committee had decided that my word was not to be believed.

Wilkes pointed out that as a member of the club he was greatly concerned as to why the meeting described to me as a management meeting turned out to be a disciplinary meeting. *"How could a meeting alter its status?"* he asked *"It can't,"* Shaw replied. *"Well why did it?"* Wilkes wanted to know. Shaw said he had no idea. *"Then perhaps we should ask"* Wilkes offered. *"None of the gentlemen here can answer that question"* insisted Shaw. Three of the senior members from that disciplinary meeting sat face to face with Wilkes, yet none made any attempt to respond. *"It is such an important question someone ought to answer it,"* Wilkes persisted but no-one offered any explanation.

Mr Shaw recommended that procedures should be changed. He was probably not aware of it but there was actually nothing wrong with the procedures already in place; the only problem here was that none of the procedures had been followed. Even so Martin Wilkes pointed out that it was the past we were dealing with and any future recommendation was of no help to Mr Baker since the disciplinary meeting had already taken place. *"We can't deal with the past,"* insisted Shaw and for reasons known only to himself went completely off at a tangent making the following remarks:-

*"This morning I played golf and missed a putt for a birdie by an eighth of an inch. I can't go back and play that hole again."* Wilkes respectfully pointed out to Shaw that his remarks were irrelevant. *"It is relevant"* insisted Shaw and followed up with *"My father died in March, can he be resurrected from the grave, can he heckers like!"* Wilkes stressed that it was a very serious complaint about a member we were dealing with.

Irrespective of the taste involved in making such remarks, I was astounded that a figure supposedly representing an advisory board, would use such analogies when trying to reach some sort of compromise regarding my being hauled in front of a disciplinary committee, without having any idea why I should have to attend.

Mr Shaw had given his assurance that he was chairing the meeting as much for my benefit as for the club but his manner and observations so far led me to believe otherwise and I was already regretting our decision to re-join the meeting.

Again Wilkes tried to go back to the original complaint, allegedly made by Derek Brown, only for Shaw to get rather annoyed, exclaiming *"tell me what it is, refer me to it. We're not playing games"* said Shaw. Wilkes pointed out that it was an allegation which Brown had subsequently denied making.

I gave Shaw an overview of the disciplinary meeting and the alleged complaint of price fixing of contracts, which Timms claimed Brown had reported. I remarked that if Brown had made such a complaint, I would have thought he would have been asked to put it in writing.

Once again the President, Secretary and the Captain, who had all been present at the original disciplinary meeting and were here to represent the committee, made no attempt to comment whilst Michael Shaw summarised it as follows, either Brown had made the complaint or he had not and that the Management Committee had reason to believe he had made a complaint. He followed this up with *"in golf clubs all sorts of things get muddled up."*

The crux of the matter was that Timms had been President. He had headed the disciplinary meeting I attended and he made the charge against me knowing there was no complaint. This did not seem that muddling to me. It occurred to me that no-one seemed keen on dragging Golf Club Presidents into disputes; despite the fact they had instigated them in the first place.

Shaw went on to state that my complaint, as it were, was with Jack Timms and Derek Brown and he wanted to know how the golf club came into it.

I freely admit I was bewildered by Shaw's comments. I did not instigate the situation, Timms did and it was he who involved the golf club by taking official action and hauling me in front of the committee. Being President gave him the opportunity to initiate proceedings and make a false charge against me, which he could not otherwise have done. The committee responsible for managing the club's affairs, as far as I could make out, were letting Timms off the hook by refusing to make any enquiry, even though they had substantial evidence to do so and Shaw wanted to know how the golf club came into it. If I had taken the golf club out of the equation and confronted Timms on a personal level, I am quite certain the club (or more to the point the committee) would not have been able to get back into it quickly enough.

Patience may well be a virtue but I was not feeling particularly virtuous towards Mr Shaw by this stage. As a means of trying to get the meeting to move on and in truth to calm myself down a little, I read out Hall's letter confirming his conversation with Derek Brown.

As Mr Brown had not made any complaint, verbal or written, I wanted to know why I was hauled before the committee when there was nothing to face the committee for.

It was a straightforward question but as before the Officers representing the committee made no attempt to answer. Shaw felt it depended on how you interpreted the word complaint; whilst Mr Duffy an ex President suggested the disciplinary hearing I attended may have arisen from a throwaway comment or jocular remark and went on to present a possible scenario. I failed to see any connection at all between 'jocular remarks or throwaway comments' and the actual allegation made of 'price fixing of contracts.' I made it clear that I had never made any derogatory remark of any kind to Derek Brown about him or Timms.

I have to confess my stomach was beginning to knot and I couldn't help thinking our initial instincts had been right.

Shaw asked *"Why then, do you feel you were hauled before the committee."*

*"I think that's what we would all like to know."* said Wilkes. I really had no idea why; that had been my reason for asking the question in the first place. Even so I explained to Shaw that although I didn't know the reason for attending, once there I felt my continuing membership of the club was in jeopardy. Shaw asked if I had any problems with the committee, to which I replied that no matter what they said, I felt I would have to agree with it.

Shaw went on to ask how I would have felt about the committee if I had not been upset and had considered myself totally 'bomb-proof.' As far as I could see this was rather a leading question which to be honest, in my opinion, had nothing to do with what we were there to discuss and I declined to answer. Shaw was having none of this and asked if I would give an honest and frank reply. This was wrong (despite his assurance that I would not be cross-examined,) I felt Shaw was now doing exactly that and I told him so. I was here trying to seek recognition that what took place at the disciplinary meeting was wrong but no-one seemed prepared to answer my questions; I on the other hand appeared to be coming under attack.

Further clarification of my so called grievance had been unnecessary. Everything had already been made absolutely clear in the correspondence. The committee were the only ones empowered by the Club to deal with disciplinary matters. They had full authority to take decisions and act on them and in my opinion, were simply passing the buck to Mr Shaw, who was not empowered to do either.

This hearing, as far as I could make out, was quite simply a damage limitation exercise on behalf of the club and I didn't think that anything Alf, Martin or I said was going to make the slightest difference. Timms would never be asked by the committee to explain his actions and the club, or more specifically in this instance, Timms and the committee would be off the hook.

I stressed that if I had not taken action to defend myself, I thought there was every chance I may have been expelled from the club. In my own mind I was sure that if I had allowed Timms to get away with this it would not have ended there.

A great deal of argument had been made about the necessity of keeping Derek Brown's letter confidential. I had no right to a copy of his complaint of me, even though just a couple of weeks prior to writing it, he confirmed he had no reason to make a complaint about me at all; yet my own letter of complaint to the committee regarding Timms' conduct had not been kept confidential. Brown was approached by the Captain, Bob Turnbull and asked to respond to it, even though Brown had already made his position quite clear.

Neither was any comment made on the fact that the disciplinary meeting I had attended had already taken place before any letter of complaint ever appeared.

Mr Shaw asked me if I stood by 'my allegations' or would I withdraw them since they were of a very serious nature. Shaw had a wonderful way with words. That had been my very question of Timms and the committee. This whole nightmare had arisen from Timms' false allegation against me and the Committee's refusal to either withdraw it or make an enquiry.

The allegation was untrue. I had said so, Derek Brown initially had said so, John Hall had said so and Derek Pinning had said so. Making false allegations about someone is an extremely serious matter, that was my whole point and yet no-one it seemed was willing to deal with it. Convincing anyone of this however was proving to be very hard work indeed.

The whole thing was wearing me down and I was becoming utterly demoralised.

Wilkes asked if any of the people present would be happy to have a disciplinary letter sitting on their file. Whilst the other people in the meeting decided to stare at their feet, John Hall did have the decency to reply *"No, but I would not take it this far."* He did not elaborate on how far he would take it, or exactly what he would have done if faced with such a matter. As you will see later in this story, he should have faced a disciplinary meeting himself. Strangely enough he did not.

The meeting moved on to John Hall's visit to my house on 17th July, where he made the proposition that if I were to drop my complaint against Jack Timms, all reference to the disciplinary meeting I attended could be deleted from the club records. Hall now insisted that he came of his own accord as a friend of mine but at the time he told June and I that he had come on behalf of the committee. Wilkes also chipped in to say that he found Hall's visit a great surprise.

Not so Michael Shaw. He stated that as a past Captain himself of a Golf Club, he would have done exactly the same thing. He saw nothing sinister in John Hall coming to see me and making the offer he did and described it as a negotiating tactic.

The meeting moved on (or back depending on your viewpoint) to the handling of the sale of the land, which had taken place several months prior to the disciplinary meeting. Alf Wragg raised the question of why my bid was not put on the notice board. Bruce Oakes, the current President entered proceedings by claiming that the bid by Philip Willers had come out of the blue. Yes it may have done but hadn't I improved on the bid? Oakes stated that it was never discussed by any management meeting that all bids were to be posted.

I read out the letters from two members of the committee; Henry Barber (handicap secretary) and Bob Turnbull (Vice Captain) confirming they had advised me that all bids would be posted on the notice board. Mr Timms had also told me the same thing.

The matter was raised as to whether the then President Mr Timms had tried to get the best price for the land.

Mr Shaw stated that Jack Timms had no duty to ensure that the club got the best price for the land. He said the only time anyone was under that obligation was when a sale was either in the hands of a trusteeship, or it was a building society repossession, otherwise it was just another commercial transaction that could be handled in any way deemed suitable. From a legal standpoint I didn't doubt that Shaw, as a solicitor, knew his facts but I referred back to the 'over my dead body' remarks, claiming that it was obvious that Timms wanted to keep me out of the bidding. Shaw's reply to this was *"Yes - what's wrong with that?"* he followed up with *"what is clear is that Mr Timms does not like you."*

I have to confess I was completely bowled over by these remarks. Jack Timms did not own the land, the golf club did, yet we were being told that it was perfectly alright for him to decide which of two bidders would get the land. I have no legal training and I may be biased but a President of a golf club was under no obligation to sell club land for the best price he could get; surely he had this duty to the club membership as a whole, if not a legal duty then at least a moral one. I would have thought that Timms was obliged to put any personal feelings he may have aside and act in the best interest of the club. Whether Timms liked me or not was surely irrelevant and it certainly did not give him the right to go around proclaiming to the only other bidder, that I would only get the land over his dead body, irrespective of how much I was prepared to bid.

*"If I was a President of a golf club and I did not like a potential one,"* Shaw said *"I would try to use my influence not to sell him the land, I find that perfectly normal. I don't agree with it"* he hastened to add *"but I find it perfectly normal."* My objections were countered

with, *"Mr Baker, does it not happen in business. You must have gone to somebody and said I'm not selling this to you."* I pointed out that we were not talking here about a private transaction but about two bidders and one plot of land owned by the golf club. *"I'm staggered!"* Martin interjected but Shaw wanted to know why, *"have you never done that?"* he asked.

I admit I was getting quite exasperated by this point. *"First you say it's wrong; then you say it's normal; so really it's normal to be wrong"* I blurted out.

Shaw went on to say that Jack Timms was perfectly entitled to turn round and say in his capacity as President that he will not sell to a specific bidder. This could be because he did not trust them or he did not like what they were going to do with the land.

Taking account of his actions so far, there was only one person in my considered opinion who was not to be trusted here and that was Jack Timms but by implication, Shaw seemed to think that his behaviour was perfectly normal.

By now Martin Wilkes, shocked at Shaw's comments, had the bit between his teeth and basically summarised what I thought but could never say so eloquently, namely that the Hillsborough Golf Club committee does not have to convey decisions to the membership. If the President decides that's what is going to happen, then that is what happens. Surely this is not in the best interest of the club he said.

Bruce Oakes decided to intervene and again stated that it was never discussed by any management meeting that all bids were to be posted.

Shaw then asked me why I had not written in to see why my bid had not been posted. Actually I did write in, pointing out my confusion on this very point but initially I had been told by the President, Jack Timms, Bob Turnbull the Vice Captain and Henry Barber the Handicap Secretary that my bid would go on the notice board, so I had no reason to doubt this. Shaw summed this up by stating that these people were clearly wrong.

I read out the letters I had written to the committee regarding my confusion of the bidding procedures, adding that I received no response to my enquiries. If bids were not to be placed on the notice board as I had been led to believe by committee members, why did no-one inform me of this and explain what the actual procedure was, I asked.

I also pointed out that as my bid had not been posted, in the interest of fair play I had advised Mr Willers myself that I had increased on his bid of £75,000.

Surprisingly, Shaw wanted to know if I had asked Mr Timms about my confusion of the ambiguity of the bidding procedure. I explained that having received the wrong information about my bid being put on the notice board, what would be the point of that.

Oakes decided to pitch in and stated that it was minuted in a Management Meeting of 24th January, that they had received a bid of £80,000 from Willers, which had been accepted. This was the same meeting where it had been agreed to write asking me if £77,000 was my highest offer.

Bruce Oakes claimed that I had made my final offer for the land, which of course I had not and that the Club was under an obligation to make a decision as quickly as possible, in order to raise capital to develop the club house.

When I heard Oakes say this I must confess I nearly choked. It was 5th August, 1999 when I initially wrote to the club with my bid. A reply from the President, Jack Timms followed on 17th August and concluded by informing me that he would be in contact within the course of the next few days. Apart from a two line acknowledgement, I heard nothing more for five months, until January 25th the following year to be precise.

If that was Oakes' definition of 'as quickly as possible' his slow decisions must be well worth waiting for.

In addition, Oakes failed to point out (and I will go into this in more detail later in the book but it is something that I wasn't aware of at the time) that at the same meeting where the committee had accepted Willers' bid of £80,000, it had also been agreed to refund him the sum of £3000 towards his costs. In other words it was identical to my bid of £77,000, where I had agreed to pay all fees myself (a condition of sale confirmed to me in the letter sent by Timms.) Also I would have been quite prepared, if need be, to increase this offer. Oakes must have known all this when he made his remarks.

By now I was beginning to lose patience with the whole process. I freely admit that if it had not been for Martin Wilkes and the presence of dear Alf, I would have lost it completely.

Shaw asked me what I expected Hillsborough Golf Club to do about it. I told him that I felt the members were probably out of pocket because they had not tried to get the fairest price for the land. They certainly didn't answer my letters. As it was I blurted out *"I do not think I was dealt with fairly for a minute."*

Martin said that if the golf club had been true to its members, then they would have gone for the best price for the land.

Shaw asked if I thought that Timms had improperly swayed the management committee. I replied that I could not say since I was not present at the committee meeting where it was decided who to sell the land to. However, in view of his clearly biased opinion and being President of the club, I did add that he was obviously in a very good position to do so.

Again Wilkes tried to find out why three committee members had told me that my bid would be put on the notice board. He pointed out that if they had told me this, which they had, then surely we must assume they are correct. Shaw said that all this indicated was that Jack Timms believed the bids would be posted. I asked him if he thought three people could all be wrong. His reply was that one person had got it wrong and he had told two other people.

I still wanted to know why the committee had not answered my written enquiries on this very issue, particularly if three prominent members of that committee had given me wrong information but their only response was… they had wanted to move on.

I had mentioned that I thought that the value of the land was possibly in excess of £100,000 and had been quite prepared to bid up to that amount. Bruce Oakes decided to ask, if I was so keen on the land, why I hadn't bid £100,000. I explained that anyone competing against a bid of £80,000 maximum would hardly increase their own bid by £20,000.

Shaw went on to say that if I was admittedly so shrewd on matters of business, why had I engaged in tittle-tattle in the bar with Timms, Barber and Turnbull? I confess I was annoyed by Shaw's comments which I found offensive. I said I didn't see how making an enquiry of the President, Vice Captain and Handicap Secretary could be classed tittle-tattle.

Shaw went on to state that he would make recommendations that the disciplinary procedures were to be firmed up. He said I should not go away feeling malevolent towards people on the committee. Malevolent was a good word, exactly translated it means wishing harm to others. I found myself wondering what word Mr Shaw might consider, adequately describes the way Timms and the committee have treated me. Shaw also proclaimed that if he had been President, then he would not have been so silly as to voice his dislike of a fellow member. He recommended that in future a smaller sub-committee handle formal business.

Who might have been on the smaller sub-committee if it had been in place when I was bidding for the land? Whoever had been on it, it seemed to me that Jack Timms would have been running it.

The meeting as a whole had taken over three hours. It seemed more like three years. I felt nothing had been achieved and the committee at the Golf Club had still failed to take responsibility for any of its actions. I went home exhausted after a thoroughly wretched time. I couldn't help wondering how Timms had spent his evening.

As a footnote to this painful exercise Mr Shaw wrote to Pigott a week later. Basically this was Shaw's summing up of the whole meeting.

*"It was clear that the principal complaint of Mr. Baker in relation to the invitation extended to him to attend the Management Committee Meeting and the subsequent letter, which followed, is the reference in that letter to a "Disciplinary Hearing."*

*After hearing the parties and reviewing the available evidence I feel from an objective standpoint that the club acted properly in acting upon the complaint in the way that it did. It was at all material times made clear to Mr. Baker that a complaint had been made and was under investigation. Nevertheless from the subjective standpoint I have some sympathy with Mr. Baker when he says, in effect, that the correspondence forms part of the record and the use of the words "Disciplinary Hearing" convey the fact that he had done something wrong, when in fact the Committee accepted that the remark was meant to be jocular."*

I simply could not make out how Mr Shaw came to this conclusion. He maintained:

*"The club acted properly in acting upon the complaint in the way that it did."*

There was no complaint; that was the whole point. There was no written complaint; there was no verbal complaint. Timms made a completely bogus and fictitious charge. This had all been explained in the correspondence and again at the tribunal. The written evidence supports this.

Shaw continued *"It was at all material times made clear to Mr. Baker that a complaint had been made and was under investigation."*

I had told Mr Shaw and Martin Wilkes had emphatically told him, that I had been hauled in front of a Disciplinary Meeting without having any idea of why I had been asked to attend. The correspondence of which Mr Shaw was given a copy bears this out.

Mr Shaw states *"the committee accepted that the remark was meant to be jocular."*

It was alleged that I had accused the President and Derek Brown of corruption involving the 'price fixing of building contracts' (a pretty serious allegation by anyone's standards.) My membership had been put at risk. My family and I had been put though a terrible ordeal. There was convincing written evidence to support that the allegation was untrue and none to prove otherwise. I had spent time and money trying to get the committee to do their duty and investigate the allegation, which had still not been withdrawn. Not once in any correspondence between the club and me was the term "jocular remark" ever mentioned.

I did not make any allegation and as far as I was concerned, none of what my family and I had been put through over the past year had been remotely funny.

Three hours of discussion and this was the summing up. It was soul destroying.

Regarding the sale of the land, Shaw had very little to say except that the decision had been made and implemented.

There was no mention in the report of Timms' assurance to the other bidder that *'Baker will get the land over my dead body'*, even though written evidence of this had been presented to the Committee at a Management Meeting and was recorded in the company minutes.

The most significant aspect of all was that nowhere in the summing up was there any reference at all to the Past President. The name Timms was not mentioned. Anyone reading the report would be completely unaware that Jack Timms had played any part at all in the affair, let alone initiated the whole thing.

The Committee had also been vindicated, according to Mr Shaw *"The club acted properly in acting upon the complaint in the way that it did"*

As far as justice is concerned, my heartfelt opinion is that my family and I had received none from Hillsborough Golf Club.

# Chapter 4

# The E.G.M

After the debacle of the meeting with Michael Shaw I was left pondering at the injustice of it all. From my point of view the tribunal had been a demoralising experience, one I am unlikely ever to forget. I know Martin feels exactly the same. We had hoped for some recognition of the injustice that had taken place; an apology, or at the very least a written assurance from the committee that there would be no further threats to my future membership.

What was the point of 'airing my grievance' as they put it if no-one was willing to deal with it. Without Timms there would be no 'grievance'. If he had not abused his position and tried to discredit me with lies and then allowed his friends to cover up for him; if he had not been prejudiced and conspired to keep me from fairly bidding for the land; in short if Timms had not discredited himself and the club by acting dishonourably, there would have been no grievance and there would have been no tribunal. It came as a great disappointment therefore that Shaw's report of the meeting failed to make any mention at all of Timms or his disgraceful conduct.

As it turned out the only ones to benefit from the meeting as far as I was concerned were the committee. It provided them with the perfect opportunity of being able to tell members that an independent tribunal had vindicated them completely of any wrongdoing and they certainly made the most of that.

With regard to the land, Shaw remarked at the tribunal that if members had been dissatisfied with the way this asset of the club had been disposed of, they were quite entitled to requisition an Extraordinary General Meeting to discuss the matter but he went on to state that they had not done so. Shaw could not have realised the level of criticism the land issue had caused amongst the club members and, however unwittingly, he had hit on one possible course of action.

I made a few enquiries and discovered that an EGM such as Shaw suggested required the support of approximately fifty of the voting members, who should be prepared to requisition the meeting and act as signatories on the requisition form. After approaching a few members for their views I was extremely pleased at the response. The comments and opinions of those I spoke to supported my own, a fact borne out by the seventy five members who subsequently put their name to the resolution in just over twenty four hours. It was positive confirmation of the dissatisfaction felt by many members at the way the sale of land had been conducted.

Anyway a notice to requisition the EGM was duly submitted to the club and basically asked that the committee carry out a full investigation into the sale of the building land at Stubbing Lane, specifically in relation to the bidding procedures followed by the Management Committee in relation to the sale; whether or not a fair procedure was followed in respect of the bidding and whether the best price which was reasonably obtainable for the land was obtained. If the best price was not obtained, whether any member of the committee acted in breach of his duty in relation to the transaction, this should include the actions of the President at the time Mr J. Timms.

The committee in their wisdom decided that the EGM was to be held between Christmas and the New Year. The precise date selected was in fact the 28th December, a time quite frankly which the committee must have realised would be most inconvenient for the majority of members to attend. Over the Christmas period people quite rightly have other and probably better things to do than concern themselves with meetings at golf clubs. If this had been the committee's intention then they were not to be disappointed. It came as no surprise at all that many members were unable to attend in person and the committee took steps to turn this to their best advantage.

Traditionally anyone wishing to vote by proxy was required to make a personal application for the form at the Secretary's Office, returning it to the Secretary 48 hours prior to the meeting. On this occasion however they sent out voting forms to every voting member of the club. They even treated everyone to a stamped addressed envelope. They obviously wanted to ensure that the maximum number of forms were returned, especially as all returned forms not assigned to a specific nominee were automatically designated to the President, Bruce Oakes.

Anyway, the members who requisitioned the EGM were permitted to include a statement of no more than one thousand words, setting out their reasons for calling the meeting. The Secretary was then required to forward this statement to all members, together with notification of the date the meeting was to be held. That covered the official requirement but the committee were not so hot on rules unless they were making them and they had their own ideas on what documentation they would send out.

The first offering on behalf of the committee was a letter from the Lady Captain, who wrote via the club to all lady members, advising them that anything other than a vote for the committee would have an extremely detrimental effect on the Club. According to her letter, she had studied all the documents and was confident the committee had investigated this matter thoroughly. She in fact urged all lady members who could not attend in person, to vote by proxy, suggesting that if they could not find an appointee of their choice then the President, Bruce Oakes would gladly do it for them. I don't know whether or not the Lady Captain was aware of it but her husband and a good friend of his had also studied the documentation very carefully and both had come to the exact opposite conclusion. Indeed they were very much in support of calling the EGM and were amongst the first to put their names to the requisition form.

The Captain, John Hall also apparently felt a compelling urge to put pen to paper and wrote to everyone on 12th December offering up his personal opinion. He informed all members that he had studied my complaint and had personally tried to resolve the matter amicably. He strongly felt that a vote in favour of the committee and against Mr Baker's resolution was in the best interest of Hillsborough Golf Club and its members.

Well that sorted me out but the Captain seemed to have lost the point that seventy five members called the EGM not Mr Baker and they were quite entitled to have the matter discussed without being bombarded with what amounted to a load of emotional blackmail.

It seemed that the message being conveyed here was 'don't rock the boat at any cost.' The facts of the matter were apparently not important, especially if they should reveal that contrary to his position, the President had not acted in the best interest of the club members. Anyway the upshot of Hall's letter was that the resolution should be voted against otherwise he too would be 'concerned about the stability and harmony of the club.'

Not to be outdone the Secretary decided to throw in his two pennies worth and also wrote giving his reasons why the members should support the Management Committee. I was under the impression that the role of Cub Secretary was to carry out the wishes of the membership as a whole and not just the committee? Rightly or wrongly Thomas Pigott did not seem to agree with this, since those who had requested the meeting were also club members. Pigott was playing a dual role and it wasn't difficult to see which hat he was wearing now. He had evidently become a committee man first and foremost.

Nevertheless, these personal opinions were all very enlightening and by now everyone had surely got the message loud and clear. Nothing should be allowed to disrupt the stability and harmony of the club; indeed every member should support the committee otherwise it would be extremely detrimental.

It was further stated that in order to prevent difficulties which may arise from a non-member of the Club purchasing the land; it was decided to offer it only to members, who would understand the restrictive covenants which would have been part of the final contract. Personally I did not understand why they wrote this. The restrictive covenant merely ensured that the club could still use the rest of the adjoining land as a golf club. As an excuse it sounded pretty lame and rather insulting to anyone who was not a member of the club. It also considerably narrowed the field of prospective buyers down to two (or more precisely one, as things turned out.)

If, as the committee now claimed, that it was never agreed that open bids would be posted on the notice board, this in association with the point outlined above merely emphasised that the committee only ever intended to sell to a bidder that suited them. No open bids, no members of the general public, (and as far as the President was concerned no Roger Baker) that left Philip Willers.

The next point brazenly stated "The terms of sale were the same for Mr. Baker and Mr. Willers." This claim was certainly not borne out by the evidence as the facts will show and to send this out to all club members was out of order to say the least.

It was also stated that the then President, Jack Timms did not vote when the decision to sell the land was reached….it was somewhat irrelevant whether Timms voted or not, he was after all presiding over the transaction and had already assured Willers that I would only get the land over his dead body.

The committee feels it carried out a full investigation and Mr Baker made his contribution at the time. Again this was so misleading. There was no investigation by the elected committee; simply a hearing at an unelected tribunal, which was not empowered to take any action no matter what contribution I made. The deal had already been done. The members were entitled to know the full facts not just the ones the committee wanted them to hear.

(The committee made no comment about the documented evidence reporting Timms' meeting with the other bidder or why the President told Willers I would not get the land regardless of what I bid. In plain English he was telling Willers the land was his. There were no other bidders. The land belonged to the members and it was the President's duty to act in their best interest. How in those circumstances could the committee justify Timms' actions?)

They then invited the membership to vote against the proposed resolution.

The committee also decided to submit the following 'extracts from documents' designed to uphold their case:

The first was Philip Willers offering £60,000 for the land "with all covenants in favour of the golf club" Willers to fund planning permission expenses himself.

The second showed Willers bidding £70,000 "The same criteria as previous offer" taking into account primary works the offer is in excess of £75,000....(what was meant by primary works or the £5,000 differential, I have absolutely no idea? Planning consent had not been granted and neither had the land been sold.)

Number three had Willers bidding £75,000.... Again agreeing to finance the application.

There did not appear to be any reason why he should keep putting in offers. At this stage (the latest entry was dated June 1999) I had not bid for the land. Willers was a builder not a philanthropist. Why keep bidding against himself?

The next entry said in nice bold letters *"It was agreed that a notice be displayed on the Notice Board allowing for objections or any further offers"*

Then came my offer to purchase the land for £77,000.....Cost of planning permission at my own expense.

A further document, apparently written sometime in January 2000 by Philip Willers, was inserted which read as follows: "Last year was generally regarded as a good year for property values and bearing this in mind I believe I could increase my previous offer by £5,000 to £80,000." At least on this occasion Willers did have reason to raise his offer, after all I had personally advised him of my bid of £77,000, which had failed to appear on the notice board.

Christmas had more or less been cancelled at our home as we waded through the reams of documentation sent out by the club to members. We had been informed of the criteria for calling the EGM and followed it to the letter. Contrary to the rules, once the committee had had the opportunity to read the statement which we had provided, they proceeded to include endless paperwork of their own, intended to try and discredit our statement.

In the run up to Christmas it would have been a minor miracle if more than a handful of members had been prepared to work their way through the endless documentation. For those who did of course, there was always the possibility that they may come across the brief statement made by the requisitionists. It could hardly be considered part of the festive activities and if the committee's intention had been to confuse the members by swamping everyone in red tape, then they achieved their aim with flying colours.

Meanwhile our own determination to scrutinise the masses of paper paid dividends. The following extract from a Management Meeting revealed the following:

<u>At a Management Meeting on 24th January 2000, it had been proposed by Ted Laycock and seconded by Henry Barber that Willers' offer of £80,000 be accepted. The club to allow £3000 toward any costs incurred</u>

Why should they allow Willers £3000 towards his costs? In effect this reduced his offer to £77,000, the same as mine. The committee had already stated that the terms were the same for both bidders yet I had not been made this offer. Their only letter to me specifically stated "All expenses in connection with the application will be paid by the purchaser."

My own offer of £77,000 confirmed that (as specified) all costs would be funded entirely at my own expense.

The committee wrote asking if this was my final and highest offer and I replied, indicating that I would be willing to increase my offer should this become necessary but to my knowledge mine was the highest bid at that time. I did however make clear that if the club had received a higher bid, I was quite prepared to increase on my offer. I received no response to this letter. Why was this if the club wanted the best price?

The upshot was that on 8th February 2000 the committee wrote letters to both Willers and me. The letter to Willers accepting his offer of £80,000 and to me they wrote as follows:-

*"Dear Mr Baker*

*The Club is now in a position to move on regarding the plot of land in Stubbing Lane. Unfortunately your final offer has been substantially improved upon.*

*Thanking you for your interest."*

Now correct me if I'm wrong but where had my offer been 'substantially improved upon' taking into account the £3000 the committee had agreed to refund Willers?

Neither had it been my 'final offer'. I had categorically stated that I was quite prepared to increase my offer should circumstances require but the committee completely ignored this.

I may have left school at 15 but there is nothing wrong with my basic mathematics. It does not need a rocket scientist to see that no matter what bid I put in (even one that Bruce Oakes or Timms would approve of) I would not have got the land. The committee had already written to Willers agreeing the deal. There were plenty of questions surrounding the whole transaction but the committee had so far refused to give any answers.

Also included was a minute from the Management Meeting of 7th February 2000 where it was agreed unanimously to accept Willers' offer for the land. That was the last minute included.

Taking account of the proxy vote issue and the misleading information already provided to the members, we felt that winning the overall vote would be virtually impossible but we were confident that if all the facts could be made public, we may at least get the support of members attending on the night. The big stumbling block was of course the President Bruce Oakes, who together with the committee would have full control of the meeting. This would greatly limit our chances of obtaining the answers to vital questions in order to get the full facts aired.

They also included a letter from Henry Barber retracting his statement that Jack Timms had confirmed that all bids would be placed on the member's notice board. An extract of this was sent out to all members, the full letter is as follows:-

*"A few months ago I was ambushed into a small statement from Roger Baker regarding a point that was discussed in committee about one year previous. The statement said that all bids received regarding the sale of the land in Stubbing Lane would be posted on the notice board. I now know that this was not the case and it was not agreed. I have searched through all my old minutes and cannot find anywhere where it was agreed that all bids would be posted. I therefore withdraw my statement from*

*Roger Baker. Please accept my apology. I should have checked before I signed."*

So according to Barber I 'ambushed' him. What exactly did I do? Stick a gun to his head? As it happens we had been chatting at the club when I asked Henry if he would put in writing what he had previously confirmed, regarding my bid going on the notice board. Henry obliged and returned the next day with the following:

*"Henry Barber*
*Handicap Secretary HGC*

*Following a request from Roger Baker I did make enquiries with Jack Timms as to whether Mr. Baker's bid of £77,000 would be placed on the member's notice board. Jack Timms confirmed that all bids would be posted and I then conveyed this information to Mr. Baker.*

*Signed H. Barber and dated 17/ 5/ 01"*

Why after six months was it decided that Henry's statement should be retracted. It had nothing to do with notes or minutes. It was simply an account of a question he asked of Timms and Timms' reply. I am sorry that Henry felt it necessary to retract his statement and can only surmise that as a member of the committee he was put under a certain amount of pressure.

Yet another retracts from his original statement. Still, Bruce Oakes liked the letter, he wrote back thanking Henry for his time and effort in establishing and verifying the situation. How kind of him. To be sure no one missed it Oakes also read out the letter at the meeting.

Finally the committee took great pleasure in informing members of the opportunity I had been given to 'air my grievances' at a meeting with Mr Shaw of The National Golf Club Advisory Association. Well that about covered it. I am sure it all made fascinating reading after a hard day Christmas shopping.

A lot of the documentation being sent to the members by the committee was clearly misleading and some was patently untrue. I knew it, some of the other clubs members knew it but the vast majority did not.

My solicitor wrote laying it on the line to the club that in effect the Club Secretary was concealing information to club members by only producing the documentation that the committee wanted its members to see. He pointed out that a requisition can only be a maximum of 1,000 words. This is limited by statute under the Companies Act. Of more importance at least from a legal standpoint the committee did not appear to have the statutory authority to send out their statement at all. Apparently only those who requisition the meeting can send out a statement not vice versa. Yet the committee had already put out numerous letters and statements and of far greater length.

Basically what we were trying to say was how could anyone be expected to vote by proxy or in person, on something where facts were deliberately being concealed? To cut this rather lengthy scenario somewhat shorter, the full document was submitted by my solicitor. He basically asked that a new date be set for the meeting and that the committee should actually send out documentation that reflected the situation in its true light and not just the one they would like to show. It was suggested that any proxies received in connection with the EGM should not be relied upon by virtue of the fact they had been induced by a flawed and misleading document.

True to form the committee refused point blank.

The date for the EGM was set and there was little we could do about it. Anyway Christmas is a time of goodwill so maybe a little of it would come in our direction.

On December 28th we turned up for the meeting. Unfortunately any thoughts of goodwill were set to disappear as quickly as they came. Within minutes of our arrival who should enter the Club and sit immediately next to Bruce Oakes on the top table? It was none other than Michael Shaw. *"What the hell is he doing here?"* said Martin but I was just as shocked as he was.

Having already endured a torrid time at the hands of Michael Shaw, the Extraordinary General Meeting was made even more extraordinary by Shaw's reappearance.

On sitting down beside Oakes, Shaw immediately immersed himself in conversation with our illustrious President. Who had invited him? Presumably Bruce Oakes but Oakes had already made it clear in no uncertain terms that legal representatives would not be allowed, yet Shaw was a qualified Solicitor. We were all members of the club so what gave the committee a special right to be legally represented when the members who had called the meeting could not be? More to the point why did they consider it necessary?

Surely this was not a meeting he should attend in any capacity. It was an EGM requisitioned by members. Shaw was not a member so what possible reason did he have to be there?

I thought it and Martin Wilkes said it and say it he did in no uncertain terms.

*"I would like to know by what authority Mr Shaw has to be here tonight?"* asked Martin. The top table seemed to be afflicted by an inability to speak. Martin pressed on *"Mr Shaw is not a member of this club and I would like to know his reason for being here."* The President and Shaw remained silent so Martin decided it was time to provide some background. He explained to those present that he had already attended one meeting at HGC chaired by Mr Shaw and based on that experience; he did not consider Mr Shaw to be either fair or impartial. He requested that unless Mr Shaw could produce some explanation or authority for being at the meeting, he would like him to leave. Michael Shaw did neither. Again Martin put his objections quite forcefully to the chair but neither Oakes nor Shaw made any attempt to respond.

The reply from Ted Laycock however was just as stringent in its tone. Laycock, who was no longer on committee, had also come in with Shaw. He turned on Martin and told him the committee could invite whoever they wanted. Contrary to his own opinion of himself, I'm not sure Laycock was too hot on the rules behind the requisitioning of an Extraordinary General Meeting. In truth he is prone on occasion to going into what I would call 'bully mode' and this was one such occasion, neither was it to be the last.

Nothing Martin, I or anyone else said made the slightest difference. Despite all objections, Shaw steadfastly remained seated and the committee maintained a stony silence. Shaw refused to either leave or give any explanation for his presence. Having issued clear instructions that legal representatives were not allowed, what would the committee's reaction have been if the members who requisitioned the meeting had brought along a Solicitor, who then refused to leave?

This attitude rather set the tone for the whole of the meeting.

The President refused to answer any of our questions. We could never have anticipated such a shocking show of blatant arrogance. Oakes' chairing of the meeting was a disgrace. He repeatedly moved the meeting on, ignoring all objections and any points of order to the chair were all waived aside.

Some members were permitted to make rude and abusive remarks from the floor without a word from those running the meeting. One even shouted "let's clear the floor ready for the New Year's celebrations." In short the meeting was a total fiasco.

June bore the brunt of a further outburst from Ted Laycock. She requested an explanation of the proposition put by him in committee and seconded by Henry Barber 'that Mr Willers be refunded £3000 toward costs for Stubbing Lane, when this was contrary to the conditions of sale set down by the club.' Laycock was absolutely furious. He spun round to face her and she found herself on the receiving end of a full scale tongue lashing for having had the audacity to question his integrity. This apparently had never happened to him before! What June did not receive was a reply to her question but she was determined to persevere.

Undeterred by Laycock's outburst, she tried once more *"Mr Chairman, could I please have an answer to my question?"* but again the President had decided it was time to move on. Evidently this subject was one that Oakes was not eager to leave open to discussion.

The President brought the meeting to a premature close despite objections that we had not had an opportunity to address the points of the resolution. The meeting was closed anyway. It was probably the shortest EGM on record.

The Meeting had achieved nothing and our questions remained unanswered.

There had been barely a comment from any committee member throughout the meeting. They could hardly have said less if they had 'pleaded the fifth.' This was obviously the planned strategy and it worked so I suppose from their viewpoint the meeting went well.

On the plus side were the kind words of support from quite a number of members and I would like to thank them. Many also expressed disgust at the way the meeting had been conducted.

I feel especially saddened by the resignation the following morning of two longstanding members; Ron Holmes, who had been a member of Hillsborough Golf Club for 27 years and his partner Jean Shepherd with about 12 years as a member. They were shocked by the heckling and sheer bad manners of some members who would back the committee regardless of any rights and wrongs of their actions. Both Jean and Ron had supported the EGM and said how sorry they were at the dreadful way we were treated. They were clearly distressed by the whole experience. Early the following morning Ron rang us at home and spoke to June. He confided that he and Jean had been so upset by the events of the previous evening they had been unable to sleep. After talking most of the night they each wrote a letter of resignation. Although they had spent many happy years at Hillsborough, after the disgrace of the EGM, they felt they were no longer able to support the club. They had delivered the letters to the Secretary's office that morning.

One other issue I would like to share regarding the fiasco that was the Extraordinary General Meeting of 2001; Andy Senior is a member who I had never met until several weeks after the EGM. He joined the Golf Club a few years previously, having served with distinction on various other committees in the area. He had read the EGM documentation from both sides and had a rather trenchant view on the subject, which he fired off to Thomas Pigott. Mr Senior has since provided a copy of his letter in which he had the following observations to make:

*"It is as a member of the company, and without prejudice, that I would ask the committee to consider the following comments and suggest a remedy to the current club predicament regarding Mr. Timms, Mr. Baker and the forthcoming EGM.*

*If Mr. G. Revitt heard Mr. Timms say that Mr. Baker would get the land over his dead body then knowingly or otherwise Mr. Revitt and Mr. J. Hall to whom he had reported the incident have not acted in the best interests of the Company.*

*It is understandable that Mr. Baker felt aggrieved when he heard of these comments and I would suggest that if these comments were never made then we would not be in the situation we are in today.*

*It is my opinion that both Mr. Revitt and Mr. Hall should have convened an emergency committee meeting to investigate the allegations concerning the alleged statement by Mr. Timms.*

*The simple facts are that both Mr. Revitt and Mr. Timms are still members of the club and this cannot be. If Mr. Timms has made the alleged comments regarding the land and Mr. Baker, then he can no longer expect to remain a member at Hillsborough as this behaviour cannot possibly be tolerated in a private limited company where every individual must act in the best interest of the company at all times.*

*If however the alleged comments were not made by Mr. Timms, in the opinion of the committee, then Mr. Revitt should no longer be a member of the club.*

*With regards to the question was Mr. Baker treated fairly regarding the sale of the land and was the best interest of the company foremost in our then President's actions, I comment as follows:*

*The President of the club has a duty to act in the best interest of the club and its members at all times. The sale of the land should have been put through a professional body i.e. an estate or land agent, without question this would have been in the best interest of the club.*

*The committee at the time should have insisted that the sale go through a professional agent and therefore they did not act in the best interest of the club".*

Mr Senior then went on to suggest a solution:

*"The obvious outcome of any further action other than the EGM will be the weakening of HGC be it financially or otherwise.*

*We as club members have a duty to act in the best interest of the club and I believe we should act as follows.*

*The land has not been sold and is therefore still an asset of the club and can be put up for sale by an appointed agent of the club.*

*Mr Baker should have an apology from HGC for the way in which the sale was handled and for the alleged comments by our then President Mr. Timms*

*Mr. Baker can contact our appointed agent and purchase the land if he is successful or still interested.*

*Mr. Timms owes HGC and its members an apology for the way he conducted himself in dealing with the sale of an asset of the club.*

*If Mr. Timms is not prepared to apologise then he should be expelled from the club immediately".*

This was pretty punchy stuff but unlike Henry Barber's letter the President didn't thank Senior for taking the trouble to send it. Whereas Barber's letter was read out in full at the EGM, Mr Senior's letter was kept well hidden until the EGM was safely out of the way.

Mr Senior had wanted the letter discussed at the EGM and had therefore sent it two weeks before the meeting. The required deadline is 7 days prior to the meeting. The Secretary, Mr Pigott did not answer the letter. No one replied to it. In fact no one had the decency to contact Mr Senior until the New Year when he was asked to go in and discuss his concerns.

True to form the letter never received a written response. How could it? It was refreshingly honest and straight forward, the sort the Committee made a habit of not replying to, presumably on the grounds 'they may incriminate themselves'. The writer as always was extended an invitation to a cosy little chat. Unlike most others who would prefer their concerns replied to in writing, Senior did go in. He was faced with Bruce Oakes, Tom Pigott and other committee members where he stood his ground and repeated his suggestions and solutions.

Senior also told Oakes, who by this time was 'throwing a slight tantrum' that he had just as much right to his opinion as the President of the Club since he paid the same amount in subscriptions - Oakes bounced out of the meeting in a huff threatening his resignation!

Thanks to the way the committee conducted the EGM, most members who attended the meeting departed from it pretty much as they had arrived 'none the wiser.' How many others like Mr Senior had challenged the committee, only to have their letters or questions remain unanswered or at best 'explained away' in private.

There is just one final issue that may give further insight into the way members at Hillsborough are misled and manipulated. Just prior to the EGM hundreds of copies of a news letter hot off the press, descended around the clubhouse like confetti. They contained the following information regarding the Potting Shed.

### _Planning Permission on the Potting Shed_

_"As members already know Planning Permission to convert the Potting Shed to a dwelling was refused, Planning Permission to rebuild as a Potting Shed was also refused and the Club is pursuing an appeal which will be heard shortly. The Club has to appeal as the Sheffield City Council Planning Department is also demanding the site be put back to a green field site._

_However this does mean that the expected £80,000 revenue for the sale of the Potting Shed will not be received and any provisional arrangements for the sale of the land have been cancelled._

_The loss of this extra revenue is a great disappointment to the Management Committee, as the loss will severely change the overall financial planning of the Club"._

Despite the opening line, members did not already know that Planning Permission had been refused; in fact this was the first time I or anyone else so far as I am aware had heard of this. Certainly Mr Senior was not aware of this when he wrote his letter to the club. Neither did the 75 members who had requisitioned the EGM have any knowledge of it. The obvious motive of the committee in deciding to make this information public at this point in time was to defeat the object of the Meeting. The committee were busy spreading the word that the sale of land would not now proceed and therefore the EGM was pointless. It did not in any way change the discrimination shown or the scandalous and underhand way the proposed sale of an asset of the club had been dealt with but I have to admit this revelation did come as a severe blow. I could well see how the majority of members would be easily persuaded that the EGM was not worth pursuing, if the eighty grand had gone up in smoke and the land was now worthless.

What this news letter did not divulge (and this was something I wasn't aware of at the time) was that Planning Permission had in fact been refused over a year earlier, on 17th October 2000 but not a word of this had been mentioned at the tribunal I had recently attended. Why was that? And why had this information been kept from the members until now, when it suddenly became in the interest of the committee to reveal it?

# Chapter 5

# The Land At Stubbing Lane

The land at Stubbing Lane on which for over 100 years stood the potting shed now lies deserted, covered in weeds and hidden from the fairway it adjoins and the reasons behind the present derelict condition is covered in this chapter. It tells a tale of how certain members of the Hillsborough Golf Club Committee for once discovered that they were not as powerful as they thought when they were forced to have dealings with people in the real world.

As I mentioned very early on in the story, all bids for the land at Stubbing Lane were subject to securing the relevant planning permission from the council, to convert the land and most importantly the potting shed which stood on the land into residential use. Irrespective of the rights and wrongs of the bidding process the land itself now lies vacant. The prospective gain of at least £80,000 to Hillsborough Golf Club can now never materialise. Sheffield City Council refused planning permission for the land on 17th October 2000.

After planning permission was refused, it would seem that the best course of action for the club would be to leave it for a while and then apply again, which they were perfectly entitled to do. Upsetting the people in the planning department is not a worthwhile exercise and would obviously hinder your chances in the future.

Nevertheless, work took place hidden under the guise of what Baldrick might call a cunning plan. If the land could not be used to build a house on, then make it an integral part of the course. In other words build something else on it, with a view to applying later for permission for it to be converted to residential use. They decided to call it a 'storage building'. In other words claim the building, which had stood empty for many years on the land, was necessary for storing equipment that was vital for the smooth running of the club.

Mr Willers proceeded, obviously on the instructions of someone, be it Jack Timms or the committee, to knock down the old potting shed with the exception of one gable end and put down new footings that were big enough to withstand a house being built on them. Those are not actually my words but can be found in a council report on the building activity that took place. Once the footings were in place, Willers continued building the structure with both door and window openings. Like many a cunning plan however this went horribly wrong once the council became aware of what was happening and stepped in.

A letter dated 28th March 2001, was sent to Willers/and Mr. J. Timms, H.G.C. by the councils Planning Transport and Highways Division. The letter confirmed previous instructions that all unauthorised works should cease immediately. Basically what Willers had done, was instead of repairing the potting shed in the original stone and brick, he had instead demolished it and erected one made of breeze blocks. This of course contravened planning laws since he was in effect putting up a new building on Green Belt land. How Timms (who is also a builder) and Willers didn't think this was going to happen is beyond me.

The Golf Club's Annual General Meeting took place on 30th March, where the outgoing President Jack Timms gave his address. Whilst this covered the usual round of thanks to the greens chairman, treasurer and the like, Timms also stated with great clarity the following:-

*"Work is progressing steadily on Stubbing Lane and by this time next year I expect Bruce (Oakes) to be announcing the successful planning application and an additional £80,000 to our funds".*

Even as he spoke, Timms knew that Planning Consent had been refused on 17th October the previous year and there would be no possibility of £80,000, or any other amount for that matter being added to our funds. Nevertheless, Jack Timms had the barefaced effrontery to tell the membership that work was 'progressing steadily'. Work was not progressing at all, everything that had been done up until that date had contravened council planning regulations. Timms was perfectly well aware of this but probably didn't think it a good idea to tell the membership, especially during his retiring President's speech.

The Council also received a letter from David Barker an Ecologist. He addressed it to the Head of Planning and had the following observations regarding the Stubbing Lane land.

*"You may already be aware that planning permission was refused for residential conversion on October 17 2000. Despite this refusal, Hillsborough Golf Club and/or Mr J.P Willers subsequently felled four trees that were of amenity value, demolished*

*virtually 90% of the buildings despite being advised that the Ecology Unit has some record of bats(a protected species) in the area, that may have been roosting in the buildings, and felled more trees and damaged a substantial part of an area of historical interest behind the demolished buildings"*

David Barker went on to state that despite both the Club and Willers being told to stop work, they had not done so.

Apparently Philip Willers had also claimed that 'as one wall remained, using the same walling materials for further reconstruction would be classed as repairs'. Barker described this as farcical, a point he emphasised further on in the letter. A substantial part of the original building was of plain red brick, wooden doors and prefabricated roofing. Since the buildings had also been abandoned for the best part of thirty years, irrespective of the building materials he was using there is no way that Willers could claim he was conducting repairs.

The local newspaper the 'Sheffield Star' it turned out had also got in on the act and ran a story under the headline 'Building not par for the course' focussing on how a Government inspector had to be called in to authorise removal of the building that had been constructed.

A further attempt to gain planning permission (for a storage building) was refused in May 2001 and by this time the Council were getting somewhat annoyed by the Club's obvious disregard of planning procedures concerning the land.

One of the local councillors wrote to the Team Leader responsible at the council for development control within the Planning, Transport and Highways section setting out in no uncertain terms what he thought of the whole affair.

*"It is quite clear that they (Hillsborough Golf Club) have embarked not only on a rebuild of the 'barn' beyond shoring up the end wall but have also put footings down and commenced building on an extension which more than doubles the original foot print. Additionally stone walls, trees and an old garden have been destroyed. What action can, and are we taking and what time scale will be involved?*

*There is considerable concern in the area that HGC are not only "out of line" but are holding the planning process in contempt. I would appreciate an early response"*

The committee could no longer ignore the council when they wrote to the club by recorded delivery in terms that even the HGC Committee would have to take notice of. After the second attempt at planning permission (for a storage building) was turned down on 22nd May 2001, the council's Planning, Transport and Highways group authorised the City Solicitor to take all necessary action, including that of enforcement and legal proceedings to secure the removal of unauthorised works at Stubbing Lane and secure the restoration of the land 'with appropriate vegetation'. Also to be taken into account was its location and the fact that it adjoined an 'Area of Natural History interest'.

The Club was instructed to remove all new foundations and follow this up by removing all resulting material from the site. The council also asked the club to comply with written confirmation of this within seven days of receipt; otherwise the club would be served with an enforcement action. Failure to comply with this is a criminal offence, a fact that the Council's Enforcement Officer emphasised at the end of the letter.

The Club Committee had argued the case that they would need the new building for the storage of equipment whilst work was in progress to improve both the 4th and 5th holes on the course. The council pointed out that the work had actually begun on these holes a year previously and no reference had been made for the need of a new storage building anywhere on the course let alone the land on Stubbing Lane.

In fact the council also went on to point out, that had the Club forgotten that initially the land, subject to planning permission which had already been refused, (was earmarked for residential property). In other words they meant the Committee were trying to take the planning department for fools but it was not going to wash down at the council. They issued an Enforcement Notice telling the club to *"restore the land in accordance with a scheme to be submitted to, and approved by the Local Planning Authority"*.

The Planning Inspectorate also received a letter from the resident closest to the land who lived at Stubbing Cottage, a Mr D. Rowett. Not being a member of the club he probably provided the best insight of anyone regarding the wheeling and dealing that seemed to be going on over the land and I have quoted his letter below:

*"I have been informed that in the above mentioned appeal Hillsborough Golf Club (HGC) have implied that it is essential that they have a storage building at Stubbing Lane. I find this extremely difficult to understand as I have lived at Stubbing Cottage, directly in front of the 'cart shed' for sixty years. When I arrived the buildings were used as workshops originally and then as storage facilities although they haven't been used as anything for at least the last twenty years which I assume is because they already have a large workshop and store close to the Club house.*

*On 17th October 2000 HGC were refused planning permission to make this building 'residential' so it would appear that essential storage buildings were not necessary at that time, and as nothing has changed in the meantime apart from a new fairway to replace an existing one there is still the same amount of land to care for.*

*It would appear that HGC are simply calling it a 'storage building' for the time being to get planning permission and get it built, and then reapply for residential whereby all the original objections i.e. 90% rebuild and removal of mature trees would not be a reason for refusal. Everyone around here can see what this is all about; the question is, can you?*

*The only reason this building is essential to HGC is the fact that with planning permission they have two customers already, one being the man who demolished the original building on March 10th 2001, save for one gable wall, laid down new foundations and started to rebuild complete with damp proof course and window openings until being reported by someone and subsequently stopped. Call it a 'storage building' if you like but the end result would be what they applied for on 17th October 2000".*

Mr Rowett was quite right, that was exactly what Hillsborough Golf Club had done. The question was who was behind it. Of course the committee would run true to form and hide behind each other but someone somewhere allowed Willers to go ahead and demolish the original building and begin construction on a new building without planning consent and they had since tried to convince the council that they needed this building as storage. All that was happening was the council were getting increasingly frustrated at the club's flagrant disregard for planning procedures.

In the run up to the 2002 AGM, correspondence was also sent to the club Secretary by club member Mr P. Gleadall.

Peter Gleadall has been a well respected member of HGC for over 30 years and is a staunch supporter of the club. He has in past years been approached on a number of occasions with a view to accepting the position of prospective Captain. Unfortunately due to work commitments at that time he was unable to accept. He has however like many others worked tirelessly for the club and is not afraid to speak his mind on matters he feels are important to the welfare of the club and its members.

Anyway on the 10th March just prior to the 2002 AGM Gleadall wrote to the club as follows:-

*"At last years Annual General Meeting the retiring President Mr. J. Timms said that work was progressing steadily on Stubbing Lane. In addition by this time next year he expected "Bruce to be announcing the successful planning application and additional £80,000 to our funds"*

*At that point in time the building known as the "Potting Shed" had been demolished. Work was already in progress on the erection of another building that was apparently erected without the benefit of planning permission, which according to a recent newspaper article the club have now been instructed by the council to knock down. We should be concerned to the fact; this new revelation from the "Star" newspaper will do nothing to enhance the expected exemplary reputation of the Hillsborough Golf Club. If this is not debated, I'm sure any future project requiring the co-operation of the Sheffield City Council Planning Department, will not be looked at in our favour".*

Mr Gleadall's letter was sent two weeks prior to the AGM. The committee however did not respond to it in writing, nor did they make any attempt at the annual meeting to explain why Timms had made such unbelievable claims in his previous year's speech, when it was clear even as he made them that they weren't true.

Peter Gleadall, having failed to receive any satisfactory answers at the AGM, requested a written response from the President to the issues raised in his letter.

With regard to one enquiry by Gleadall, Bruce Oakes did have the wherewithal to write *"The cost of the building work already carried out and the cost of demolishing these works will be done by Phil Willers at his own expense with no cost to the Club"*.

Without residential planning permission Willers had no need for that land, so why had he been given permission to demolish the original Potting Shed and start building on the land when planning consent had not been granted?

Gleadall had followed up by questioning the potential loss of £80,000 to the club.

The President's response to this enquiry was priceless. He explained it away by saying: *"With the full support of all members we may have succeeded in obtaining Planning Permission"* well thank you for that pearl of wisdom Mr Oakes, so it was actually the fault of members that planning permission was refused. Unfortunately Oakes didn't attempt to explain by what reasoning he came to this amazing conclusion. He even followed this up with *"It is regrettable that members who were obstructive are not like Phil Willers and contribute to the club"*.

Oakes failed to mention that by flaunting planning regulations in the first place in demolishing the original Potting Shed, along with it went any possibility for future planning applications and as Gleadall quite rightly stated; the potential loss of £80,000 to the club.

Bruce Oakes had also added diplomacy to his financial skills and knowledge on building matters. Whilst he was perfectly entitled to sing the praises of Philip Willers if he so wished, he seemed to have forgotten that he was singing them to the same Peter Gleadall who had devoted a lot of his own time working for the benefit of the club. Gleadall had been 'House Chairman' at a time when the Club did not have a Steward. Not only did he supervise the staff but he also did the relevant shopping, organised the bar and its associated supplies, looked after the cleaning staff and did the ordering. This was in addition to his full-time job.

My apologies if I digressed from the original purpose of this chapter but I was merely trying to highlight once more how there seemed to be a two-tier membership coming into being at Hillsborough Golf Club, which meant that you either had favour with the committee and ultimately the President or you did not. Peter Gleadall with his straightforward approach and his unwillingness to creep around the powers that be belonged firmly in the latter.

At the 2002 AGM meanwhile, Bruce Oakes (who according to Timms would by now be announcing the successful planning application and a boost of the club's funds to the tune of £80,000) was instead attempting to explain to the membership the reason the venture had failed.

Oakes stated (not for the first time) that if every member had supported the planning application they would have stood a better chance of it being granted. (This seemed to be a favourite phrase of the President.) Precisely what the granting of planning permission had to do with members he did not say, especially after the Timms and Willers double act had already gone around building on the land without planning permission anyway. Nor could I work out who this rather snide remark of Oakes could be directed at. Just for the record however, any member of the public can request to view all documentation relating to a planning application, as I did myself whilst researching this book. I suggest Mr Oakes does likewise. He will find no objection to the relevant application from me or any other Hillsborough Golf Club member that I am aware of.

Anyway not content with this, the President invited Mr Willers to come up and make a speech.

Willers stated he had been up against too much opposition. Well I suppose when faced with neighbouring property owners completely fed up at the flaunting of building regulations and local council officers actually insisting that planning authority be obtained before the start of construction, not to mention ecologists concerned with bats and the like, you would feel somewhat threatened. Willers apportioned blame to councillors, local residents, everyone except himself and those who gave him permission to flaunt planning procedures. He made no mention that all this opposition had been self inflicted as a result of cutting down trees and erecting a building without permission. That must have slipped his mind in the face of all the pressure he was under from everybody opposing him.

# Chapter 6

# A Friendship Lost

John Hall and I went back so long that I doubt either of us can remember when we first met. As a child I lived on Thirwell Road, Heeley and John lived 100 yards away on Goodwin Road. When June and I first married we lived in a small terraced house in Dronfield on the outskirts of Sheffield. With the birth of our first son Russell, we moved and renovated a two bedroomed terraced at Darnall, renting our first house to John's mother and father, Gwen and George. John's brother Graham worked for me for many years. His sister Janet has been married to my brother David for over 40 years. To put not too fine a point on it we were close. Everyone in the respective families was friendly with each other and even when my family moved to Derbyshire I still kept in touch with the Hall family and at weekends John and his sister Janet would come and visit us. When I returned to Sheffield as a teenager we basically started up where we had left off and I often popped in to see John's parents.

John and my brother David, along with two other members of the Golf Club bought an apartment in Spain a few minutes walk from ours. If we happened to be on holiday at the same time we would meet up for a meal or drinks and have the occasional round of golf. It was on one of these occasions that June suggested to John's wife Christine, as she walked with us around the course, that she ought to take up golf herself and June volunteered to be a sponsor on her application. At home we frequently socialised and dined with the Halls at the club.

Until the start of my dispute with Hillsborough I can never recall us being anything other than the best of friends. As you will have already seen this relationship became stretched by the events of 2001 and completely collapsed in March 2002. This was the culmination of a number of incidents and two in particular.

The first was so breathtakingly ludicrous that even now I cannot believe the cheek and downright arrogance of it. I will refer to this matter in other parts of this story as well but it bears being outlined here to explain to some extent, believe me I cannot explain it all, how the friendship did totally collapse.

After the fiasco of the EGM in December Ricky, June and I realised there was nothing to be gained by banging our heads against a brick wall. It was a hard pill to swallow, knowing certain individuals had abused their position and got away with it. Not just concerning the land, but more importantly on a personal level. I had been lied about, had a trumped up charge made against me and generally been the victim of prejudice and vindictiveness. Worse still, others had covered up for those responsible, no doubt under the guise that they were 'acting in the best interest of the club', when really it was their own selfish interest they were thinking of.

Anyway as a family we had decided it was time to return our energies to the more enjoyable task of playing golf.

The following months passed uneventfully and to be honest it was a great relief not to receive any letters from Hillsborough Golf Club. The peace however came to a sudden halt and just as things had settled down events took on another turn. Out of the blue I received a telephone call from a well meaning member of the club. It was approaching the Club's Annual General Meeting, which took place each year at the end of March and apparently a notice had appeared on the clubhouse notice board stating the following:-

**Dear Mr. Secretary**

**At a meeting of Past Captains and Past Presidents held on Tuesday 5th March 2002 the following Resolution was agreed :-**

**"Proposed that Mr. R. Baker be required to reimburse the Club for the legal costs £2,400 incurred in defending the integrity of the Committee against his accusations in several letters from his Solicitors.**

**The Committee has received overwhelming support from the membership. Should Mr. Baker refuse this requirement then action be taken under Article 16."**

**The resolution should now be submitted to the A.G.M. to be held on Monday 25th March 2002."**

Listed at the bottom were the names of those attending the meeting. The wording of the notice gave the impression that all had been in favour but I was later to discover that this was not the case.

Anyway the resolution had been sent to the Club Secretary and was put on the notice board for all to see.

Not a word had passed between the committee and me since the EGM the previous year, yet without a word of warning here I was being publicly threatened with expulsion under the now infamous Article 16.

Contrary to what the notice claimed, the shoe was in fact on the other foot. It was my integrity and not the committee's which had been brought into question. What a strange phenomenon it is, that on acquiring a title or position, some folk suddenly consider they have more integrity and are more deserving of respect than the rest of us. They don't seem to realise that these qualities are earned and cannot be given along with a badge or a title.

I could barely believe the arrogance of it all. There would have been no solicitor's fees for either me or the club if it were not for Timms playing god. The committee were as bad; they could have held a proper enquiry and cleared up the matter straight away instead of covering up for Timms and persecuting me. Brown's own assurance to Hall and the further confirmation from Derek Pinning that I had made no derogatory remarks about Timms or Brown should have been enough to clear my name and resolve the matter.

It seemed inconceivable that having already escaped all accountability for their actions, these same people should choose to resurrect matters once again. Someone was seriously determined to have me out and one thing was certain, it had absolutely nothing to do with legal fees.

The threat of expulsion was becoming a regular practice. The Club's very first solicitor letter almost a year earlier, in April 2001 had ended with just such a threat. If it had been justified, the committee would have followed it through at the time? After all there were no legal fees for the club at that point. If Timms and the committee had done nothing wrong why spend £2,400 of Club funds in 'defending their integrity?' The obvious answer is they wouldn't and it is even less likely they would have squandered that amount of money if it had come out of their own pocket.

Anyway it was further proposed that this Resolution be submitted to the Annual General Meeting to be held on March 25th.

This latest development in any event had come as a total shock, especially as the Secretary had not written to me about it. It was perfectly clear that money was not the real motive here. The committee knew I had no obligation to pay their legal fees and if they felt I owed them money, the obvious thing would have been to write and ask for it.

It was also claimed on the notice that the committee had received overwhelming support from the members. This was more brain washing techniques. How could they make this claim when like me, the first the members knew of the resolution was when it appeared on the notice board? How had the membership managed to show this overwhelming support? Unless the committee were telepathic, making this claim was quite simply a downright lie.

If one was to take a light hearted view it could be said that I was finally getting something on the notice board. It was not really what I wanted up there however, allowing all and sundry to see that the Golf Club was demanding money from me. Evidently not everyone wanted matters resolved between me and the club and this twisted scheme was just another way of re-opening them. So who exactly were these Past Captains and Presidents who felt that I owed them money?

Most notable of all was of course Jack Timms; if anyone at all was responsible for the club's legal fees (not to mention my own) it was Timms himself. Without him there would be no fees, there would have been no dispute and just as thing had begun to settle down, here he was on another crusade to get me out. He was like the pied piper of Hillsborough, one peep on his whistle and everyone jumped to his tune.

Another member of this friendly gathering was none other than Timms' friend and go-getter, Bob Turnbull as well as my old pal John Hall. John in fact was still serving Captain (not a Past Captain at all) and had no real cause to take part in this latest scheme. I could barely believe what was happening with John and here he was sticking another knife in the wound. Anyway he evidently wanted to show his support for this most worthy cause. Ted Laycock was another of the old gang to make a resurgence, along with a couple of others who had all been at the Disciplinary Meeting where Timms was first given a free hand to fabricate lies about me and which started off this whole nightmare in the first place.

It was obvious that my decision to let matters drop and get on with my life had not been the outcome some had anticipated. This latest resolution hadn't simply come out of the blue. It had been carefully thought up and organised and it didn't take a member of mensa to figure out who was behind it. Life was beginning to feel a bit like 'groundhog day.'

I later discovered from one of the Past Captains who had been invited to the meeting, that it was in fact chaired by another of the original brigade, the current President Bruce Oakes. Presumably he preferred to remain anonymous as his name was not included on the list of those who attended.

Past Officers have no statutory powers within the club. The resolution they had proposed had no official standing and should not have been placed on the member's notice board at all. One other serious aspect of this was that whilst the Club Secretary made no attempt to notify me about the resolution, he had no reservation at all in putting it up on the notice board for everyone else to see. If this had been a genuine attempt to recover money they felt I owed them, then contacting me would obviously have been the first move.

Not everyone at that meeting actually agreed with their pronouncement however and I am extremely grateful here to Mick Byrne, a past Captain, who contacted me to advise that he for one had attended the meeting and was totally against it. Byrne had firmly opposed the resolution and was extremely upset that his name was put on the notice, giving the impression that he had in fact been in favour of it. He strongly objected to re-opening matters, especially after what had happened at the EGM. Following this episode he made it his business to read up on all the correspondence between me and the club and has since given me his full support.

To say that I was angry and upset with John Hall was a serious understatement. He was not a past Captain so why attend the meeting? He had thrown away a lifetime of friendship and backed a resolution by a made up committee, intent on getting me out of the club and publicly embarrassing me and my family in the process. I had treated John's own boy Christopher, like a son when he first joined the club as a teenager. June and I took him to Woburn to see his first professional competition and I generally kept an eye on him. John didn't get to the club as often in those days, working out of town as he did. Now he was a big shot in the club and his response was to subject my own son to this kind of public humiliation. This final act was the last straw. Since the notice was displayed at the entrance to the main lounge, it could not be missed by anyone who entered the club. Members, staff and even visiting members from other clubs could all immediately see that I was apparently in debt to the club to the tune of £2,400, which I had to repay or else! The wording of the notice also gave the distinct impression that I (and not Jack Timms) had been the one to make accusations.

At the forthcoming Annual General Meeting, John Hall was due to stand down as Captain having served his term, I will leave you to decide if it was with honour and distinction since I guess by now you know my opinion. John, who seemed reluctant to relinquish his newfound niche on the committee, had put his name forward for re-election; in fact it seemed ironic that the notice proposing John as a candidate at the forthcoming election for committee, sat side by side with the notice he had supported proposing my own expulsion. With the AGM looming I put pen to paper. As always I addressed it to Thomas Pigott.

The main thrust of my letter concerned the telephone conversation John had had with Derek Brown and that having established that the allegation made by Timms at the disciplinary meeting was untrue, John did not use this information to clear my name but chose instead to help cover up the actions of Mr Timms.

The letter continued:-

*"It is a documented fact that on 17th August 2001 Mr. Hall visited myself and my wife at home and made a proposition to destroy all company minutes relating to my appearance before the committee in August 2000, if in return I would be willing to drop my complaint regarding the allegations made against me by Mr. Timms.*

*In these circumstances I strongly feel that it is inappropriate for Mr. Hall to put up for re-election and would expect that he do the honourable thing and withdraw".*

Quite frankly John's behaviour towards me was now bordering on the inexcusable. He knew I would never agree to pay the club's legal fees and the meeting had merely been a sham, quite simply another excuse to be rid of me. I was devastated that John had played a part in it. It came as no surprise at all that the committee saw things somewhat differently and I received the following from Bruce Oakes the President:

*"Your letter was discussed in full at the Management Meeting held on Monday 18th March and it was unanimously agreed that your letter was*

*without foundation."*

Quite frankly I did not share the committee's views. If John Hall and indeed the committee in general had acted honourably, then I certainly had not heard about it. The incident that followed a few days later should help you decide if John Hall could actually be cited as 'acting honourably'.

On March 21st, June and I dined at the club with my brother Tony and his wife Anne. Early on in the evening I had been chatting with John's wife Christine at the bar, she had in fact approached me to try and find out why my friendship with John had apparently disintegrated.

I explained to Christine that she only had to read the notice board which was just a few yards away to answer her question. If she really wanted to know what was going on, I said she was more than welcome to read all the facts for herself of everything that had taken place. I don't think Christine had any idea of what John had been getting up to, or that he'd thrown away our years of friendship to please the people on the committee and show what a jolly good 'Captain and team player' he was. It certainly goes some way towards providing some sort of explanation for what happened next.

The following is a letter written by my brother Tony to the Club documenting what occurred that evening:

*"I would like to describe to you an incident that took place on the evening of Thursday 21st March. My wife and myself were dining in the restaurant at Hillsborough Golf Club together with my brother, Roger Baker and his wife June. At about 11pm we*

*were the only diners left in the dining area when Mr
John Hall came storming up from the lounge area
and shouted at Roger, saying "You, I've just had
enough, I want you outside, I'm going to have you."
We all sat there dumbfounded at this outburst, then
Mr Hall shouted again whilst leaning over the table
into Roger's face "outside, I want you outside, I'm
having you." I thought that Mr Hall was going to hit
Roger until Mr Phil Willers came up to Mr Hall and
pulled him away from the table. Mr Willers escorted
Mr Hall away from our table and out of the club. A
few minutes later Mrs Hall came over to our table
and said that she was sorry about John's behaviour.
We then left the club at about 11.25pm.*

*My wife, Mrs Anne Baker is in full agreement with
the above description of this incident."*

I had not in fact spoken to John for several weeks as in
the circumstances least said, little hurt seemed to be the
best policy. Had Christine confronted him about our
conversation earlier in the evening? Short of asking
John, which I fear would now be impossible, I will never
know.

The next morning my brother Tony saw John at the
Club talking with the President and informed John that
he was reporting the incident of the previous evening to
the committee.

I also informed the Secretary of the Captain's conduct
and provided my own written account. Since Hall had
already put forward his name for re-election to the
committee, I asked that this serious complaint be
discussed prior to the AGM. I received a reply a couple

of days later from Club President Bruce Oakes, confirming that the matter would be discussed at the next Management Meeting.

I heard nothing more until the Honorary Secretary deigned to reply a month later.

Pigott actually wrote that 'all complaints have to follow the correct procedure.' Well I have to admit it sounded quite good in theory. Anyway this apparently meant that the incident could not be dealt with prior to the Annual General Meeting, which by the time I received this letter, had already taken place anyhow. What exactly the procedure is for a Club Captain who goes around threatening members with physical violence in the dining room in front of witnesses was not explained.

The enquiry was to be conducted by Pigott and the latest recruit to the ranks of the committee, none other than Hall's best friend and successor as Club Captain, Mr Garry Revitt. The committee obviously saw no problem with this as there were numerous other committee members who could just have easily taken on this task.

Although Hall had admitted the complaint regarding his conduct, he had not seen fit to withdraw from the elections. Bruce and the rest of his committee chums had kept Hall's seat warm so it was business as usual. In the circumstances no-one needed a crystal ball to forecast the outcome of the enquiry into Hall's conduct. It was apparently time for his back to be scratched. The whole business made me sick.

The eventual decision was conveyed to me in a letter from Pigott on 7th June 2002 the contents of which I quote below.

*"Dear Mr & Mrs Baker*

*Re: Incident on Thursday 21st March 2002 and your letter dated Thursday 23rd March 2002.*

*After evaluating the details of the investigation regarding the incident involving yourselves and Mr. J. Hall, the Management Committee has asked me to convey to you their decision.*

*Following a discussion with Mr. Hall and reading your correspondence, the Committee felt there was no need to take any further action and consider the matter now closed".*

Well thank you Mr Pigott for that long awaited official notification but let's be quite honest here; as for the matter now being closed, was it ever open? John Hall was presumably given the nod the morning after the incident, when he and Bruce Oakes were having their cosy little tête-à-tête. How else could Hall be allowed straight back onto committee, let's face it he has already proved where his loyalties lie. Having done his share of sweeping things under the carpet it was now time for his friends in high places to return the favour.

If Hall's actions had taken place in the local public house he would most likely have been barred but not at Hillsborough Golf Club, where I think it is fair to say, only the rank and file members have to abide by the rules.

My brother Tony put everything in a nutshell that fateful evening as we left the Club. He said that despite the intense pressure I had been under, if the situation had been reversed and I had behaved as John had done, the committee would have hung me out to dry. They would have convened an emergency meeting faster than you could say 'Article 16'. It's highly unlikely there would have been any investigation at all but in any event the outcome would have been a foregone conclusion. Regardless of the circumstances, if I had lost control there would have been no excuse.

# Chapter 7

# The Public Notice

My heart sank at the thought of another battle with the powers that be at Hillsborough. I realised by now that it didn't matter how much right you had on your side if no-one was willing to deal with it, it was pointless banging your head against the proverbial brick wall and my head was still sore from the last round.

It was infuriating that having escaped all accountability for his actions, Timms was actually party to this latest witch-hunt. If there was any justice at all, it would be his name and not mine displayed on that notice board.

Anyway the resolution had been sent to the Honorary Secretary and posted on the notice board without anyone having the courtesy to notify me first.

Of course no-one reading the notice would doubt the truth of it, why should they? They were not to know that those proposing the resolution included people who had already conspired to have me out and others who had condoned that behaviour by letting them off the hook. Perhaps the committee had hoped this would be the final straw and I would resign in disgust. To be quite honest, I felt like doing just that but to walk away now would send out the message that I had done something wrong, leaving those responsible free to add whatever spin they chose to the damage already done.

I was already heading the bill in the gossip stakes; everyone was talking about it, not only Hillsborough club members and staff but visiting parties from other clubs. In fact everyone who walked through the clubhouse doors couldn't fail to see what a dreadful character Roger Baker was. It was obviously intended to cause the maximum embarrassment and I have to admit it certainly did that.

The club is situated in the heart of the local community where I have lived for over 30 years and news spreads quickly, especially when it is displayed across a public notice board. Unfortunately the only means I had of defending myself was to write to the same people responsible for the notice being displayed.

It was a terrible situation but I felt worse for my wife and son, who had to endure the gossip and whispers every time they entered the clubhouse. It would have been easier to avoid the place altogether but again I suppose that was their intention. It was difficult to believe this kind of thing could happen in a golf club where we had once thought of everyone as fellow members and friends or at least friendly acquaintances. They had no right to plaster my name on a public notice board as though I were a common criminal. I am not a violent person but by this point quite frankly, resorting to physical violence would have seemed a welcome release. Unfortunately I would have had to suffer the consequences. You will probably realise by now I didn't have friends in high places that would cover up and whitewash things for me.

Anyway I had no alternative; I had done nothing wrong and I wasn't about to resign or just sit back and let them kick me out without a fight. I had studied the club's 'Articles of Association' and couldn't see anything that entitled them to put me on a notice board like some bad debtor, or threaten to publicly expel me if I didn't pay them a sum of money which they had never made any request for in the first place.

I had to find out whether or not they had a legal right to make these threats.

Solicitors well versed in Company Law didn't come cheap but I needed expert advice and couldn't see what other choice I had. Fortunately my suspicions were confirmed. It turned out that I had no obligation to pay the club's legal fees and they had no right to threaten me with expulsion.

The main point to be clarified was why such a statement had been put on the notice board in the first place. The committee were asked to identify exactly how they came to the decision that I was liable to pay costs which they had incurred, since I had accepted no liability for them and had no legal obligation to do so. They were also asked to clarify exactly how I had done anything injurious to the club that I should be threatened by Article 16.

The Solicitor made it clear that the placing of the notice would cause other members to hold me in lower esteem and was therefore defamatory. He pointed out that the company's rules would not allow the resolution to be submitted to the Annual General Meeting and requested confirmation that it would be withdrawn. In any case it was requested that the notice be removed with immediate effect and replaced with an apology.

The reply from the President, Bruce Oakes was short and to the point.

*"The Annual General Meeting will proceed for the will of the membership to be expressed at that meeting.*

*Mr. Baker is entitled to attend and make such observations as he thinks fit: indeed we will be delighted to see Mr. Baker at the meeting".*

How typical of his arrogance! The President didn't seem to care whether the resolution or their intention to put it to the AGM was a breach of company rules or not. His reply was written on behalf of the club members, concerning a matter of extreme importance but in keeping with his predecessor, Oakes believed that his own prejudiced opinion should take priority over his duty as President.

I was tired of being used as a punching bag by the powers that be at Hillsborough. It was obvious the committee wanted me out at any cost. The Articles of Association which they were so fond of quoting went out of the window when it suited them. I could cite numerous occasions where the conduct of certain Officers could be considered injurious to the club but the rules didn't apply to them and even if they did, there was no-one to enforce them. There was no independent panel to investigate the conduct of Officers or Committee Members and if one thing was certain, it was the knowledge that they were completely incapable of doing it themselves.

Anyway Bruce Oakes apparently would be delighted to see me at the AGM? Well that would be something different since he had not so far been keen to make any other observations that would have aided my cause.

Strange as it may seem, despite the arrogance of the letter sent by Oakes. He subsequently denied all knowledge or responsibility for the resolution, or the posting of it on the club notice board, placing all the blame on the Past Captains and Presidents.

Unfortunately Oakes' short letter did not address any of the concerns raised. Was the AGM (despite it had no basis in law to do so) going to vote on whether I should pay costs or indeed whether the Committee intended to invoke Article 16.

Would the President be so arrogant if he and the committee he represented were prevented for once from hiding behind their position as the Management Committee of Hillsborough Golf Club and were held personally responsible for any legal costs arising from proceeding with the proposed resolution.

It was time to spell out a few facts and this was done the next day. My solicitor again pointed out to Oakes that if the committee tried to pass a resolution getting me to pay costs, the Club would be in breach of procedures outlined by the Companies Act. It was also pointed out that if any costs were incurred by me in trying to stop these issues getting on to the AGM agenda, then I would go to Court to get them reimbursed and that (due to the Committee's flagrant breaches the Members of the Committee should be ordered to pay the costs personally.)

It took until the date of the AGM, 25th March to receive a reply. The committee, or whoever was responsible for the decision making, apparently didn't fancy the idea of dipping into their own pockets and despite Oakes' previous letter, it was acknowledged through their Solicitor that the resolution requiring me to reimburse the club for legal costs would not be put to the AGM.

The other issues raised however were not addressed at all. Neither was there any apology for the notice or for the humiliation it had caused me and my family and acting in their usual cavalier fashion the committee still did not remove the notice until two days after the AGM. This ensured that it was still on display on the busiest night of the year, by which time everyone who had entered the club had managed to take a good look, gossip, form opinions and do what comes naturally to people in large gatherings. Anyone who may have missed it had it pointed out to them by the committee's lackeys.

Oakes even blatantly stated at the AGM that "due to one person the proposed resolution could not be voted upon." He didn't bother to explain to members that the Company Rules would not allow the resolution to be submitted to the Annual General Meeting, nor did he mention his own arrogant response when advised of this and the possible consequences his intended actions may have had.

Anyway by this point the committee had basically taken on the mantle of the three wise monkeys, stating through their solicitor that "the Club Committee were not involved". Well of course they were involved; no amount of legal argument, twisting the English language or indulging in New Labour spin could alter that fact.

It was totally beyond me how they could claim such a thing when considering the following points:

1. The President Bruce Oakes chaired the meeting at which the resolution was proposed, despite the fact his name did not appear on the list of those present.

2. Two other members of the current committee (the Captain, John Hall and immediate past Captain, Bob Turnbull) also played their part in the meeting.

3. Only the Secretary or someone sanctioned by the committee is permitted to post notices on the club notice board.

4. The notice claimed that the committee had received overwhelming support from the membership for the resolution. As the members were not aware of the resolution prior to the notice being posted, this was an impossible claim to make, although it did provide further proof of the committee's involvement.

5. The notice quoted the amount of legal fees I was expected to repay. Only the committee would have access to this information.

6. Those attending the meeting were advised of it via the Secretary's office.

7. The Committee placed the resolution on the AGM Agenda.

I was sick and tired of the lies. True to form no-one involved was willing to own up and take responsibility for their actions. The committee had full control of the club's affairs; how could they possibly have the effrontery to claim that this latest travesty had nothing to do with them?

In financial terms my legal costs arising from this shameful episode amounted to over £2,000 and I imagine a similar amount for the club. In personal terms the unnecessary humiliation and heartache caused to my family was something that couldn't be measured. Unfortunately I didn't have the luxury of putting up a notice demanding the reimbursement of my legal costs as the club had done. Neither was I in a position to threaten Article 16 even though their conduct warranted such action.

In view of all that had happened, it was quite astonishing that the committee should continue to cite my conduct as injurious to the club. If those responsible had any honour at all, they would have taken their own advice and put pen to paper there and then and written their own letters of resignation. I hardly think they could teach me anything about honour. They should have examined themselves first to see if they had any, or at least a conscience and the guts to stand up and say (what we are doing to Roger and his family is wrong.)

Ultimately the committee refused to accept any liability, either for the terrible ordeal they had put me and my family through, or for the substantial costs I had incurred in getting them to withdraw a resolution which had no right to be on the AGM agenda in the first place.

The members would foot the bill for the committee's mistakes whether they were aware of it or not. I finally took the decision to make one last effort to try and resolve all the various issues by suggesting a round the table meeting and it was to this end that I instructed my solicitor to send the following letter:

*"Whilst our client still feels aggrieved by the way in which he feels he has been treated by the club and in particular by the notice which appeared on the club's notice board shortly before the AGM in March. He is willing to consider whether a basis for settling the various issues can be found without the necessity and cost of litigation which he would be reluctant to pursue".*

Ten days later we received notification that the Club intended to expel me under Article 16. The committee did not want to have a meeting; they just wanted to have me out of the Club and on Wednesday 11th September, I received a letter from Thomas Pigott at the bidding of the powers that be advising me of the following:

*"The Management Committee have instructed me to inform you that they are considering passing a resolution to expel you from Membership of the Club under Article 16 on the grounds that you have been guilty of conduct injurious to the club. You are therefore requested to attend a full committee meeting at the club on Wednesday 18th September 2002 at 7p.m. in order for you to make a response".*

*"At this meeting you will be allowed to be accompanied by another member of the club, who is not a Solicitor. You will be entitled to make any verbal or written explanation of your conduct and put forward your defence before the resolution is put before the committee.*

*In view of the history and allegations made against the committee it is the intention that if the procedure results in expulsion, the committee will ask the membership via an E.G.M. to endorse the resolution.*

*Therefore we have taken the opportunity of enclosing a pack of correspondence, which the committee will have before them at the above meeting, and to which you may respond".*

The die it seems had been cast.

# Chapter 8

# The Expulsion

So I faced expulsion from the club I had played golf at for more than 15 years. How did I feel? Well shocked, depressed and most of all angry.

I could of course have resigned instead of waiting to be kicked out as the committee had so kindly suggested but why should I? I had done nothing to warrant resignation, unlike some who had every reason and what of my family and other members who had fought so hard on my behalf. It would amount to admitting I had done something wrong and justifying the committee's actions; even so if I had had any inkling at all of the shameful events that were to transpire following my expulsion, my family and I would have gladly walked away without a backward glance but more of that later.

It was quite remarkable how a committee who had consistently failed to convene a meeting to question Jack Timms about his well documented misconduct, was suddenly able to gather the troops to expel me with such exceptional speed.

How so many issues involving Timms could have gone unanswered was impossible to comprehend. Not just his biased conduct in connection with the sale of the Stubbing Lane land but the fiasco with the planning department and the farcical saga of events involving the Potting Shed, which was now lost for good and the inexplicable speech Timms made to members announcing the expected funds of £80,000 when he knew planning consent had already been refused. The false allegation that I accused him and Derek Brown of corruption; I know after my telephone conversation with Brown that he never made this claim. Last but by no means least, the disgrace of the public notice and the humiliation that it caused for me and my family. Timms once again was in the thick of things. How they could demand money from me claiming it was spent 'defending their integrity' doesn't bear thinking about but that of course was just another ploy. The real intention had been to get me out and now they had succeeded.

I could well see from the committee's point of view, how expelling me was the ideal solution. This latest escapade had backfired and they had dug themselves into a hole. With me gone they could wipe the slate clean and close the book on all these issues; I suppose I was the perfect scapegoat.

The procedure for expulsion at Hillsborough Golf Club is perfectly straightforward. The Management Committee vote on the expulsion and that is it. You either stay in or you go. As you will see on this occasion they also decided to have their decision ratified by calling an EGM. This is not standard practice and had probably not happened before but the committee evidently felt they needed the backing of the membership if for some reason things didn't go to plan.

I realised that the outcome of the Committee Meeting on September 18th was clearly a forgone conclusion, since the panel deciding my fate included people who had already proved they were willing to do anything to get me out. Considering my relationship with some committee members by this stage, it was obvious I could not possibly get a fair hearing. Anyway it was suggested to them, that all committee members who had been actively involved in the dispute should not participate in the discussion, voting or decision making process on my expulsion.

I had consistently appealed to them to act impartially and investigate the actions of Timms and Brown and they were clearly biased against me. We also requested that the meeting be tape recorded, or at least a full transcript be produced. Just in case anyone was interested, it was also pointed out that the Club had actually produced no evidence on which it could expel me. If the Management Committee had further evidence (although I knew already that there wasn't any) then they should produce it. Needless to say none was produced.

It was during this period in the run up to my expulsion that a number of letters were written to and from the committee in connection with the Timms/Brown affair.

Below is a letter from Derek Pinning together with the Club's reply.

*"To the Committee H.G.C*
*24th May 2002.*

*Dear Sirs,*

*As the Committee know, in July 01, I wrote a letter confirming that I had never witnessed Mr R Baker accuse Mr Timms or Mr Brown of price fixing of contracts or any other form of wrongdoing.*

*In October 01, I wrote again about the allegation which had been made against Mr Baker but I never received a reply.*

*Several weeks ago I wrote again to the Committee and still never received a reply. I have seen a statement signed by Mr Hall which says that Mr Brown denies making a complaint against Mr Baker and I find this totally confusing. Could you please explain this?*

*It seems to me and I would think anyone else taking time to read the same facts that Mr Timms or Mr Brown have tried to discredit Mr Baker and as I said in my last letter I would like to know if they have been before the Committee to explain their actions and if not why not?*

*Mr Baker had to face the Committee even though he had done nothing wrong. As I didn't receive the courtesy of a written reply to my previous letters, I would appreciate a written reply to the questions above as soon as possible.*

*Thanking you*

*D. P. Pinning"*

On May 30th 2002 the following reply was received:

*"Dear Mr Pinning*

*Your letter dated 24th May 2002 was brought to the attention of the Management Committee on Monday 27th May 2002 and they have asked me to invite you to a meeting with the President and myself*

*in order to answer points raised in your letter.*
*Please contact the Secretary's office at your earliest*
*convenience to arrange a date.*

*Yours sincerely*

*T.C. Pigott*
*Hon. Secretary"*

Pinning replied. He pointed out that his questions were very straightforward. He thanked Pigott for his offer but maintained that since he had not received any response to previous letters, he would prefer a written reply as requested. Pinning of course did not receive a reply, how could he? There was no explanation, certainly none that could be put in writing.

Martin Wilkes wrote several letters in a similar vein but inevitably came up against the same brick wall. His last letter written on July 5th 2002 was addressed to Pigott, the main points of which are copied below:

*"It is puzzling why the Management Committee*
*seem unable to answer straightforward questions*
*from a member. I would not be asking these*
*questions had the answers already been given to Mr.*
*Baker as you suggest. Can you please advise me of*
*the dates of the letters in which the following*
*questions were answered.*

*1. Why Mr. Timms has never been called before the*
*committee so that a thorough investigation can*
*be undertaken concerning Mr. Baker's alleged*
*remarks to Mr D Brown.*

2. *Does the committee agree that unless and until Mr. Timms is called before such a meeting and the outcome made known to all members Mr Baker cannot be asked to pay any legal fees as all the legal fees incurred by both the club and Mr Baker may have been avoided if such a meeting had taken place many months ago as Mr Baker requested".*

The usual offer of a meeting with Pigott and the President was declined. What Martin wanted and I expect you can guess by now he didn't get, was a written answer to his straightforward questions.

My own success rate was no better. The Club's solicitor had written:-

*"Our client's position is that the Committee will give your client a fair hearing"*

A fair hearing! As sure as eggs were eggs it would be another of their unanimous decision jobs. Every decision the committee took seemed to be unanimous. The one thing I had consistently not been given was a fair hearing and if there was one certainty in this world, I was not about to get one now.

The committee refused my solicitor permission to attend the hearing. They had admitted to spending thousands of pounds of member's money in legal fees; the latest funds squandered as a consequence of the public notice and the resolution which they had to abandon. Despite that, they stated 'this is not a meeting of a legal nature.' The presence of a solicitor was something only they were entitled to when it suited them, as on the occasion of the EGM called by the members; neither were they keen for the meeting to be taped but instead the club would arrange for someone to take full notes of the hearing and to produce a transcript in due course. Pointless as it turned out since they never bothered to provide me with a copy.

Minutes were meaningless anyway if they could be altered or deleted to benefit the situation as past experience suggested. So I should face the committee with one trusty sidekick. That was not something I would force on my worst enemy. Whoever I chose would most likely end up next in line as having inadvertently committed some serious misdemeanour.

My solicitor insisted on making one final attempt to at least get the meeting adjourned. He argued that I needed legal representation so that my case could be heard fully. He was of the opinion that if he wasn't permitted to attend the meeting there would be little point in my facing the committee alone. It was put to them that the Club was being unreasonable in denying me this. It was also pointed out that the Club had not proved that I had done anything that could be considered injurious and therefore any decision to expel me would run contrary to Article 16 of the Association. To conclude this line of argument it was put to the Club that if they could not prove any wrongdoing then how could they expel me?

All I really felt now was an overwhelming sense of sorrow and anger. Sorrow for what my family had been put through ultimately for nothing. I felt angry because I was going to be beaten by these people, who had covered up for their own and had got away with it by hiding behind their position. Anyone having the courage to write in was either ignored or invited in for the cosy chat routine. In the real world as individuals they would have been accountable but here collectively they were a law unto themselves. I suppose I could have felt sorry for myself but what was the point in that? I had tried to do what was right and ultimately I had to concede defeat to those who held all the power.

During the course of that afternoon I thought long and hard and came to the same conclusion as my solicitor. What could I possibly have left to say to the committee that they didn't already know? Those who had consistently refused to convene a meeting for the purpose of clearing my name were now more than happy for me to attend one but not for the reason I had envisaged. It was a bitter pill to swallow.

So the Management Committee Meeting on this occasion took place without me and on its conclusion, that great bastion of the letter writing industry, the Honorary Secretary Thomas Pigott sprung immediately into action. His letter came as no surprise to me, my wife and sons, my friends or my solicitor. It was dated the day after the committee meeting and read as follows:

*"The Management Committee have instructed me to inform you that the Resolution "that Mr. Roger Baker be expelled from the membership of the Club under Article 16 being guilty of conduct injurious to the Club" was proposed and seconded at the meeting held at the Golf Club on the 18th September 2002.*

*This resolution was carried unanimously and therefore your membership of Hillsborough Golf Club has been terminated forthwith".*

I expect you enjoyed writing that Mr Pigott.

So I was no longer able to play the sport that I loved with my friends and family. Moreover as a golf club outcast neither could I play elsewhere even if I wanted to, which just at this moment in time I didn't. To be perfectly honest I felt shattered and I needed time out as they say to take stock after all that had happened.

The only hope I had left was to put my case as best I could to the forthcoming EGM which fortunately was due to take place as soon as possible.

# Chapter 9

# The Ultimate Disgrace

It was my first day as an ex-member of the golf club and as you can probably gather it was not an enjoyable one. I doubt anyone, other than my family, could imagine the sheer frustration of it all. I was stunned more than anything by the speed at which they had managed to organise and carry out my exit. The Committee of Hillsborough Golf Club had finally done their worst, at least that's what I assumed; regretfully I was about to discover how excruciatingly wrong I could be. That very same day whilst Thomas Pigott was beavering away at my official 'you're out of the club letter' my son Ricky was already in the throws of becoming the next of the Baker family to fall victim to the powers that be at Hillsborough. Perish the thought he should be given even one day's grace before the vultures swooped.

This is an account of June and Ricky's story. Throughout the whole of their ordeal and an ordeal is what it was, my wife and son have acted with extreme restraint and dignity and refused to be cut down by the sheer vindictiveness of the people who now targeted those closest to me. Ricky and his mother are both of a similar quiet nature, as I'm sure everyone who knows them would agree. It would be fair to say, they are the most unlikely people to be involved in controversy of any kind.

The story I have to tell makes my blood boil even as I think of it. I imagine most parents would agree that raising a family is not the easiest of tasks but I have to admit that with Ricky, June and I have been lucky. He has grown into a normal, friendly and likeable young man. He is by no means perfect but like his brother he works hard and has never caused us any serious problem worth mentioning. It is natural therefore that I should feel sheer disgust and downright anger at the events which subsequently took place.

The last couple of years had been extremely unpleasant to put it mildly. At times we had felt like screaming at the injustice of all that was happening but had kept our own council and gone along without blowing our top or doing anything that could be construed as behaving improperly and in the meantime had tried to get our concerns dealt with through the proper channels. There had never been any hint of a complaint regarding our conduct from any ordinary member of the club; nevertheless Ricky and June especially, were to encounter what can only be described as the ultimate disgrace.

Having played golf with his usual crowd Ricky had just entered the club with his playing partners. They made their way directly towards the men's bar and ordered a drink. The group had barely sat down when for reasons best known to himself, Garry Revitt, the Club Captain suddenly jumped from his seat and came marching across from the other side of the room. Prodding Ricky on the shoulder, Revitt loudly exclaimed *"look here, I am not having you staring at me like that!"* and proceeded to have a go at Ricky in front of everyone. It was quite extraordinary, especially as the bar was busy at the time and quite a number of people witnessed Revitt's outburst. Ricky had in fact been sitting facing the bar and not being blessed with eyes in the back of his head had no view of Revitt at all. Some members were quite perturbed at Revitt's actions including Tony Fletcher, a former Captain, who witnessed the episode and later told Revitt that his actions had been out of order. Those around Ricky also expressed complete surprise at this uncalled for outburst.

Ricky was extremely annoyed and embarrassed by the whole episode. Taking account of the fact that I had only been expelled from the club the previous day, Ricky simply told Revitt that under the circumstances he thought he might have acted with a little more dignity.

Despite being a little on the quiet side, Ricky is good natured and easy to get along with. He enjoys a bit of friendly banter with the lads but I have never known him have a serious argument with anyone at the club, it just isn't in his nature, so he was naturally upset by Revitt's actions and decided to make a hasty retreat. Ricky called in to see us on his way home and was clearly distressed by the whole incident. It had been humiliating for him and I could well imagine how difficult it had been not to retaliate. It was my first day out of the club and it must have been hard enough on my son without Revitt rubbing salt in the wounds. Whether he was trying to get a rise out of Ricky I'm not sure but if so he had picked on the wrong person.

It was something we hadn't been aware of at the time but Revitt was in fact keeping notes, a kind of little black book if you like, in which items were logged and stored for later. Anyway we were subsequently informed that the official term for this is the 'Captain's Report' and apparently is an integral part of a Captain's duties. No one we knew had ever previously heard of such a thing but the committee said this was so and who were we to argue?

All the same, I hadn't yet had time to fully digest the implications of my own predicament and already my son was being singled out for the unwelcome attentions of the power brokers of Hillsborough. Revitt's actions meanwhile did nothing at all to improve his own image; taking advantage of his position as Captain to throw his weight about in public did not exactly endear him to other members. There was no further comment from him however regarding his apparent sensitivity to being looked at and as far as Ricky knew that was an end to the matter; Revitt on the other hand had other ideas and had already mentally jotted it down in his Captain's log.

Two days later Ricky was on the 1st tee waiting to play golf in the regular crowd. Only two or three others had arrived on the tee at the time, one of them being John Standrin, who had taken charge of conducting the draw for partners. Having been aware of the recent incident in the men's bar, it had been natural to assume that both Ricky and Revitt would have a more enjoyable game in separate groups and John invited Ricky and another member to tee off first, which made perfect sense. Innocent as this seemed at the time, unbeknown to Ricky, John or anyone else for that matter, the Captain, who was surveying matters from the practice putting green, apparently saw things differently and decided this was the perfect opportunity to make another entry into his Captain's log. Oddly enough, if Revitt had any problem with this, he never raised it with anyone at the time and neither Ricky nor anyone else could have known that once again the Captain's sensitive feelings had been offended. Even so, this could barely be described as an incident as nothing actually took place, except in Revitt's mind of course but needless to say it would emerge in due course.

Moving on to the following week, my wife June and her golfing partner Eric Liddell were by chance drawn against the Captain and his wife in the semi-finals of the club's mixed foursomes knock-out. June is of the opinion that if you are entered in an official club competition you accept the draw and get on with it. Mrs Revitt however had an entirely different view. Earlier in the golfing season, she and her partner refused to play in the next round of a club competition after being drawn against June and her partner in the ladies knock-out.

On that occasion they informed June's partner, Sheila that whilst they had nothing against her, they felt they could not play with June. This was apparently due to my problems with the committee, of which Mr Revitt was of course a member. Anyway Mrs Revitt had not spoken to June since that time and it came as a great surprise to June therefore, that Mrs Revitt had agreed to participate in this game at all.

In any event, Eric and June chatted before the match and agreed that in the circumstances, making small talk would be rather difficult. They decided to concentrate their efforts on the game in hand and resolved to let their golf do the talking, so following the initial pleasantries there was naturally very little conversation other than the occasional polite comment of 'good shot' etc. Everyone seemed to be concentrating on their game as all four were playing well. Having initially been two holes down, June and Eric managed to win four of the next five holes to go two up in the match by the half way stage and the game seemed to be progressing smoothly. Precisely at this point however things took a turn for the worse.

The Captain indicated to Eric that due to June's lack of conversation, she was making his wife uncomfortable and suggested June should make the effort to chat more in order to put Mrs Revitt at ease. He asked Eric to pass this message on. Revitt was well aware that his wife had not spoken to June for months, so what his motive was in passing on this message was highly dubious anyway.

The two ladies had been on every alternate tee together and Mrs Revitt had made no comment to June about her apparent discomfort; in fact for nine holes there had been no social conversation at all between the two, which was hardly surprising. What would they have to talk about? So whilst the men were taking their drives from the 11th tee, June referred to the message she had been given. She asked why Mrs Revitt hadn't said anything to her direct if she had a problem. June pointed out that halfway through a semi-final knock-out was hardly the time to complain about lack of conversation; after months of not speaking, it was obvious they were not about to walk around the golf course making polite social chit-chat. These comments didn't go down too well with Mrs Revitt, who became rather irate and launched into various complaints of her own. The Captain's wife was annoyed to say the least; not to put too fine a point on it, our problem with the committee had apparently put a complete damper on her husband's year as club Captain. Anyway the exchange ended with an agitated Mrs Revitt refusing to continue with the match. June replied it was her choice and she could suit herself.

With that Mrs Revitt marched off and made her way towards the men's tee and June followed on behind. On reaching her husband Mrs Revitt suddenly burst into tears. By now she was throwing a slight tantrum and hurling various accusations at June. It wasn't quite what you would expect; just the same, June had no intention of carrying on a slanging match in the middle of the golf course and whilst this commotion was taking place, she and Eric stood by in silence. The Captain did his best to calm his wife down but his efforts seemed to have the opposite effect. Her shouting became louder and she accused June of swearing. Not prepared to put up with this, June firmly denied the accusation but Mrs Revitt wouldn't stop shouting and proceeded to throw in the odd expletive for which June was blamed, since according to Mrs Revitt, she had said the same words earlier. It was quite some minutes before the Captain was able to restrain his wife and calm her down. June and Eric meanwhile remained in stunned silence. Needless to say at this point the match was abandoned.

June was naturally upset by the day's events and on returning to the clubhouse, she immediately rang and asked if I would collect her as soon as possible, commenting only that the match had been abandoned. Eric understandably had been of the same frame of mind as June and had also made a hasty retreat. Meanwhile the Captain and his wife, who had evidently made a remarkable recovery from her traumatic experience, were once again on the first tee preparing to venture back out onto the golf course.

I collected June's golfing equipment from outside the professional shop and was out of earshot in the car. As June left the clubhouse to join me in the car park, the Captain was already striding down from the first tee towards her. Revitt, whose size and build resemble that of an overweight rugby player, was now shouting and throwing his considerable weight about. He yelled at June that I was barred and demanded that I get out of the car park. June told him that I had come to collect her and if he had any problem with this would he please put it in writing. Revitt's parting shot as he strode back to the tee was "don't you worry, I will be writing to you and about you."

The image of Revitt throwing his substantial weight about with a woman of June's slight frame was not one to contemplate. Nothing of what had happened however was revealed to me until we were safely back home. Revitt meanwhile wasted no time at all in carrying out his threat. Saturday afternoon or not, Revitt must have reported immediately back to Pigott, who found no problem at all in putting in a bit of over-time to help out one of his committee buddies. They were after all a seasoned double act when it came to handling complaints; the evidence of this of course was their investigation of the John Hall incident.

Once June had calmed down, she rang Eric and was amazed to hear that Pigott had already sprung into action and had spoken to him at home about the incident, instructing Eric to write down his account of the day's events. Imagine the Secretary's response if any ordinary club member had contacted him at his home on a Saturday afternoon to complain of an argument during a mixed knock-out.

All the same, June was extremely upset and annoyed by the whole affair. She said that the only person with cause to complain about the day's events was her and not the other way around. Eric had already outlined his account to Pigott and replied that as the only independent witness, he was sure his account would put an end to the matter. Eric however had been speaking from the point of view of a normal logical thinking person. He was not accustomed, as my family were, to a committee hell bent on proceeding with complaints, despite not having one jot of evidence to support them.

I had been out of the club for less than two weeks and already June and Ricky had been on the receiving end of complaints, both courtesy of the same family. If it wasn't so upsetting it would be farcical. Within days the rumourmongers were at work and offensive stories began circulating around the club that June had been swearing at the Captain's wife. No prizes for guessing the source of the rumours. Eric had also been confronted with the rumours himself in the men's changing room. It was extremely upsetting for June, the stories weren't true but the damage was already done.

Meanwhile a complaint had been received by the Lady Captain, Audrey Watts who wanted to know if June wished to make a response. Naturally June did but she would first need to see the letter of complaint setting out exactly what it was she had been accused of. June could hardly believe that Jean Revitt had made a complaint, after all it was she who had abandoned the match and proceeded to make a scene in the middle of the golf course.

The 'mixed gruesomes' (a term jokingly adopted for this type of competition) had reputedly produced hundreds of arguments over the years, some much more serious than this but never to my knowledge had one ever resulted in an official complaint. The match had been abandoned and in normal circumstances that would have been an end to the matter. It was obvious that the ego inflated Captain Revitt wanted to make more of it; hence his phone call to Pigott straight after the match but June had done nothing wrong. Eric, a former President himself, had given his account to Pigott and expected the matter would then be dropped. There were no other witnesses, so why should Pigott and indeed Revitt proceed with any complaint?

June subsequently learned from Audrey Watts that she could not have a copy of the complaint unless Mrs Revitt gave her permission, which evidently she did not, as despite several requests June was refused a copy of what Mrs Revitt had written about her. I realise this is familiar ground but if the letter was true what possible objection could Mrs Revitt have for refusing June a copy? Surely the victim of the complaint is the one person most entitled to see it. How else is it possible to make a proper response?

Mrs Revitt's letter apparently was for the eyes of the Management and the Ladies Committee and June had no right to receive a copy. Instead in a letter sent by the Ladies Committee she received brief extracts of what the letter contained, that June had allegedly used abusive language and she was asked to reply to the allegation in writing or attend a meeting with a ladies sub-committee, at which she would be entitled to take another member with her if she wished. There was no mention at all of Mrs Revitt's antics on the course.

The letter producers at Hillsborough were once again firing on all cylinders. June was informed that the club were proceeding with the complaint, despite the fact the complaint was based on Mrs Revitt's word alone and June had already said it wasn't true. Obviously June's word didn't count and Mrs Revitt's did and just for the record, if anyone was interested, the only evidence of anyone swearing and making a scene on the course had been the Captain's wife herself. If by chance this news hadn't been distressing enough for one day, the Management Committee with their wonderful sense of timing decided to follow this up with another blow, which even by their standards was completely below the belt.

The next letter of glad tidings to greet us that day was addressed to me personally from my old pen pal Pigott who wrote as follows:

*"The Management Committee have instructed me to inform you of your position with regards to visiting the club.*

*You will be treated as any other member of the public when visiting Hillsborough Golf Club. Any member of the public who visits the club does so under the restrictions; that such a visitor is allowed onto the Club's grounds and premises only at the invitation of the Management Committee.*

*I therefore inform you that as from Friday 11 October 2002 such permission for you to visit the Club's grounds and premises has been withdrawn".*

Pigott had certainly put his best literary efforts into this one. The Management Committee (including Revitt) was well aware that following my expulsion, the only 'visits' I made to the club car park were to drop off and collect my wife from golf. These guardians of the club's grounds were also aware that being a one car family, the only person to suffer from their petty rule enforcement would be June.

Consequently since that time we have to unload June's golfing equipment on the main road at the bottom of the drive, from where she has a further up hill trek of around 300 yards (golf clubs etc in tow) in order to reach the clubhouse.

This latest situation had obviously come about as a result of Revitt's tantrum as June left the club after the ill-fated match. I sincerely hope that Revitt, (whose wife incidentally also relies on being dropped off in the car park) and the rest of the committee decision makers at Hillsborough, who went along with this disgraceful show of self righteousness, feel suitably proud of themselves as they continue to pass June on their way up and down the drive.

I had been out of the club barely three weeks. My expulsion had not yet been ratified by the members but it seemed that the maximum pressure was being brought to bear on June and Ricky to 'persuade' them to leave. I felt devastated. My wife and son had done everything they could to support me and now they were being persecuted as well.

The rumours about June meanwhile were still circulating the club. I could only sympathise, having been through it myself I knew exactly how frustrating it was.

With correspondence from Hillsborough now arriving on all fronts, June (to put it mildly) was at an extremely low point and because of the allegation Jean Revitt had made, she felt she had no option but to make a complaint of her own which she had not intended to do.

Despite having done nothing wrong, June was wary that Revitt's position as Club Captain placed her at a distinct disadvantage. There were no illusions any more about the absolute control held by the committee, or the fact that some officers took advantage of their position. The whole affair was preposterous; nevertheless it was causing June a great deal of distress.

Unbeknown to either of us at that time the committee were already planning ahead. A Management Meeting had already taken place on October 21st. At this meeting the committee voted to authorise a new bylaw, giving them the power to suspend a member 'pending investigation'. Formerly suspensions were practically unheard of and then only on proof of serious misconduct, which in my experience had only previously happened once. This however was to become an integral part of June's ordeal. Taking part and voting in that meeting was John Hall and of course Jean Revitt's husband Garry. Once again we were about to enter into more painful correspondence with the illustrious Thomas Pigott.

June meanwhile had agreed to meet with the ladies sub-committee to answer Mrs Revitt's complaint. The rules permitted her to take along another member and she approached Pat Woodland, a Past Captain to ask if she would be willing to take on the task. All due credit to Pat she agreed without hesitation. After reading the correspondence, Pat was astounded that the club were actually pursuing the matter at all. It was simply a case of one person's word against another, what possible justification could there be? Pat also pointed out to the Ladies Committee that June was noted for her quiet disposition and was definitely not the sort to go around causing controversy.

There was nothing in Eric's statement to suggest that June had done or said anything wrong, quite the opposite in fact and the complaint was based entirely on Mrs Revitt's word. When Pat further discovered that June had been refused a copy of the complaint she was astounded. June and Pat raised all of these points at their meeting. The secrecy surrounding letters of complaint still rankled with June, especially after the Derek Brown affair and she wrote to the Ladies Committee objecting to this practise but the Lady Captain confirmed she was only following the directive she had been given.

Pat Woodland argued that there was no evidence against June at all and to proceed with the complaint was pointless. It could only increase the speculation and gossip, adding to the stress June had already suffered. The Lady Captain, Mrs Watts said the Complaints

Procedures had to be followed. She had been advised, which I'm sure she had, that every complaint once made must be investigated. This had not been our experience; despite the undeniable evidence in the serious misconduct of Jack Timms, no amount of complaints had compelled the committee to investigate him.

It was obvious to any independent person that this was just another witch-hunt. As far as June's conduct was concerned there was nothing to investigate. The ladies on the sub committee were sensible enough to realise this. Anyway the meeting had gone reasonably well and the Management Committee would be notified of the ladies' findings. Naturally June was hopeful that her ordeal would soon be over; the downside of course was the malicious gossip, which we were unable to do anything about. Both June and I are extremely grateful here to Pat Woodland, not only for the help and support she gave at the meeting but for her continued friendship and support since that time.

Meanwhile, on Saturdays for many years there had been a regular gathering of the same people to play what in golfing terms is known as a 'fiddle'. Basically this is just a group of members who meet and draw for partners. This term however has taken on rather a different resonance to me over the last couple of years but as it was called a fiddle I will stick with the name.

By way of background here, following John Hall's attack on me in the club restaurant, the next time John and Garry Revitt (who had now followed in Hall's footsteps as Captain) turned up to play in the regular group, I had made it clear to them there was no way my

165

family could be expected to play golf with John Hall again. John had to be thick skinned to have turned up in the first place after what he did and I didn't see any reason why we should drop out of the group we had played in for many years. John did not turn up to play in the group again whilst I was in the club. He played instead with Garry and other friends and there had been no further problem.

Anyway this Saturday was only the second of these fiddles to be played after I had been expelled and it came just a week after the disastrous match against the Revitts, where the complaint had been made against June by the Captain's wife. In fact I will endeavour to entwine both stories since there are many crossovers between the two and this will help show exactly how the committee made up rules and regulations to suit themselves.

The usual crowd had turned up to play. Some of the group had already set off and still remaining were Ricky, June and two others members, Richard Lomas and Alan Bray.

The Captain, Garry Revitt also arrived on the tee, accompanied by John Hall and having nicely got me out of the way, were clearly intent on rejoining the fiddle. They were in the company of another friend, Phil Yeardley. Anyway this quite clearly put both June and Ricky in an awkward situation as they had previously made perfectly clear their position regarding John Hall, a state of affairs that still bothered them after John was another Club Official to be let off, following his serious violation of the rules.

Phil Yeardley had obviously been designated to draw for playing partners and June, faced with a potentially embarrassing situation, especially after her dreadful experience the previous week, decided to avoid any further problems by dropping out of the fiddle altogether and she quietly told Phil that she and Ricky would play on their own at the back of the field. Apart from trying to avoid an awkward situation, June assumed her suggestion would satisfy Garry Revitt, as it meant that John Hall could re-join the regular group and she and Ricky would have no alternative but to drop out permanently.

Hall made no comment but Revitt, who clearly understood the implications of turning up on the tee with Hall in the first place, refused to let the matter drop. Making the most of the situation he walked over to face June, Revitt said her behaviour was disgraceful and went on to accuse her of imposing her prejudices on others. It was clearly an embarrassing situation for June, especially in front of everyone and she was left with no choice but to respond. She asked if Garry had really expected her to play golf with John, when he had threatened to assault her husband in the Club dining room and no action had been taken. Ricky had kept silent but was obviously not prepared to stand by and listen to his mother being called disgraceful, and told Garry he should know all this as he helped whitewash the incident. Under normal circumstances he wouldn't have voiced his opinion but what Ricky said was quite true. John Hall had admitted the incident; no action had been taken and it was Revitt and Pigott who conducted the investigation which resulted in the committee deciding to do nothing.

Richard Lomas then suggested that Garry tee off in

front with Hall and Yeardley and he and Alan Bray would play behind with Ricky and June. The Captain's parting shot was to publicly accuse June of embarrassing the other members. Both Lomas and Bray were shocked by the incident. It was not how you would expect a Golf Club Captain to speak to a lady member, especially in front of her son and other members.

Hall and Revitt already knew when they turned up on the tee, that June and Ricky couldn't possibly be expected to play golf with John Hall and why should they? Other than club competitions, people are quite entitled to choose who they wish to play golf with and as for Revitt; surely he wouldn't choose to play with someone, who only one week earlier had allegedly sworn at his wife. I'm equally certain that John Hall did not wish to spend three hours strolling round the golf course with my wife and son, or vice versa. The whole incident was clearly stage managed and there was no justifiable reason for Revitt having caused such an unpleasant scene. Nothing more was said about the incident at the time but later that day June told the rest of the group that as Revitt and Hall were to re-join the fiddle, she and Ricky would drop out of the group altogether.

By the beginning of November Pigott's letter writing skills were back in full flow, the recipient of the correspondence having now switched to Ricky.

Pigott wrote *"The Management Committee have instructed me to inform you, that after receiving information from the Captain with regards to comments you have made at the Club, together with your general conduct at the Club you are requested to attend a meeting to allow you to comment on these allegations"*

Needless to say Pigott did not go into any detail of what 'information' he had received from the Captain but judging by the allegations that were made against Ricky it had not been particularly complimentary.

Ricky was accused of the following:

*"Your general attitude towards Officers of the Club in the men's bar on 19th September"* Pigott's improvisation of the 'staring incident' was quite understandable. 'You are accused of staring' does not quite have the same ring.

Second up was *"not acting in an acceptable manner as a Golf Club member by refusing to play in a game of golf with the Club Captain on September 21st 2002".*

Ricky was baffled by this one. It was just two days after the staring incident and Ricky knew he had not refused to play golf with Revitt.

Finally in connection with the John Hall/Garry Revitt affair Ricky was charged with *"accusing the Captain of whitewashing an investigation regarding a complaint against another member"*

Whenever the John Hall incident was raised the committee never referred to him by name, he was always 'another member' as if by omitting his name somehow made him less guilty. Anyway there was little point in denying this one, he had done it and what son wouldn't have lost his cool with the giant Revitt hovering over his mother and calling her disgraceful. What Ricky had said was perfectly true but that had no bearing I suppose. The committee didn't seem to hold much store with people who told the truth.

Anyway Ricky was summoned to attend an investigation of his alleged actions with three members of the Management Committee as well as a fellow member of the club if he so wished.

Ricky replied, pointing out that the events complained of dated back quite some time. He recognised from the date that 'His general attitude towards Officers of the Club' must relate to the staring incident but he had not refused to play golf with Revitt two days later and could not recall any incident. Ricky also wanted to know what was implied by 'his general conduct at the club' and who had made this complaint? Of course no-one had made it because it wasn't true. It had simply been thrown in for good measure. It was a phrase I recognised as having been thrown at me on several occasions without any good reason. Pigott evidently could not think up a reasonable explanation as Ricky's general conduct was not mentioned again.

It took until the beginning of December for them to reply with anything substantial. Pigott claimed the delay was because he had to collect evidence from other people, evidence he did not include with the letter he sent to Ricky. He had already had six weeks or more prior to advising Ricky of the complaints but it had obviously not occurred to Pigott to obtain the evidence before proceeding with the charges. This would have been especially helpful considering the first two complaints were baseless trumped up rubbish. Revitt himself should be facing charges for having made them.

Whilst Pigott didn't provide answers to the questions

Ricky had put; he did decide this would be a good time to quote extracts from the Captain's Duties. Actually Pigott did include, I assume unwittingly, some rather amusing and ironic pieces on the Captain's role.

*"At all times the Captain should make himself available to the members and listen to their complaints and suggestions".*

*"In the event of petty differences between members try to keep an open mind and be fair if expressing an opinion".*

This last quote was priceless, particularly as the former Captain had tried to assault me across the dining table. The current one meanwhile had brought charges against my son for staring at him and had branded my wife's behaviour disgraceful in front of other club members. Revitt appeared to be conducting a personal vendetta against both my wife and my son, not to mention his wife's complaint, which based entirely on her word, had resulted in an investigation.

I think this might well be an appropriate time to re-write the script of the 'Captain's role'.

Ricky was summoned to attend and still he had not been presented with a shred of hard evidence or written complaint other than the brief outline in Pigott's original letter. A meeting was fixed for December 16th which Ricky had no choice but to attend or 'it would proceed without him.'

June offered to go with him but apparently this was not permitted and since I was persona non grata, Peter Gleadall kindly stepped into the breach. Even the committee realised that this was one meeting where John Hall and Garry Revitt could not be in attendance so the meeting was chaired by Revitt's Vice Captain, Mr Graham Watts an ex. police sergeant. Also present was Mr Brian Shaw, (rather ironic really as both could be classed as neighbours of Ricky, living just yards away from him on the same street. Both Watts and Shaw incidently also have sons of a similar age to Ricky.) Making up the threesome was of course Thomas Pigott.

The week prior to the meeting, Brian Shaw made a visit to my home after being unable to contact Ricky direct. Brian (whose son, David is also a club member) has known Ricky since he was a young boy. He was concerned that Ricky should make the right responses at the enquiry and wanted to discuss this with him. Brian talked about the incident concerning June and Ricky on the first tee. I asked Brian how David might have reacted if Revitt had publicly insulted his mother in front of him. Brian did have the decency to admit he thought it was a disgrace. He confided that he had no time for Revitt, who he didn't see eye to eye with at all.

Brian Shaw had originally been co-opted onto the committee mid-term and I asked him why he didn't resign when he admittedly knew what was happening was wrong but the answer as from others I had spoken to was always the same. It's not that easy. What could be so difficult about saying …"this is wrong - I resign?" Brian said he tried not to get involved with the politics of the club, claiming his only interest was in the building projects. I told him that Ricky had done nothing wrong and could only tell the truth at which point Brian left.

I cannot begin to express the level of disgust I feel that

Ricky was obliged to attend this hearing to answer such piffle. Every day in the newspapers you read about car thieves, thugs, vandals and worse and here at Hillsborough Golf Club, someone who had grown into a decent level headed young man was being made to jump through hoops, for no other reason than he was my son and yet again the complaints having come from a committee member.

Ricky attended and answered all the allegations in the best way he could. As regards the first and most ludicrous of the three, that Ricky had been staring at Garry Revitt, prior to the latter coming over and being aggressive, Ricky basically stated that as far as he was concerned he had found the whole situation embarrassing, not just for himself but for other people present in the bar at the time. Les Morton who had been sitting with Ricky at the time of the incident gave his written account. Morton confirmed that he and Ricky had just entered the men's bar. They had both got their drinks and sat down with the rest of the fiddle. Within minutes the Club Captain had approached Ricky from the opposite side of the room and said in a very aggressive voice: *"I am not having you staring at me like that"* Ricky replied, *"I am not staring at anyone I am just going to have a drink".*

Morton also confirmed that the bar was quite full and a number of people who play in the fiddle were perturbed at this outburst from the Club Captain and Tony Fletcher, a former Captain stated his disapproval concerning the incident to Garry Revitt at a past Captain's meeting.

Ricky referred to the comments made by Mr Fletcher but Graham Watts, who was chairing the meeting, had the unbelievable audacity to rule Fletcher's comments 'inadmissible as hearsay evidence!' I have to say this completely bowled me over.

Here we have a former police sergeant, who throughout his career must have dealt with criminals of every description and was now relegated to conducting an enquiry that my son had allegedly stared at Revitt. What a trial it must have been for Watts when a witness statement from an ex. Captain had to be ruled 'inadmissible as hearsay evidence'. Excuse my sarcasm but the whole preposterous affair simply beggars belief. How could any committee possibly justify proceeding with complaints such as this?

I could well see how the committee had been too embarrassed to ask the Past Captain, Tony Fletcher to substantiate his 'hearsay evidence' in writing.

It seems very sad now but a number of years previously, June and I had welcomed Audrey and Graham Watts to stay with us in Spain when they had been unable, at short notice, to find a suitable holiday. We spent a very enjoyable week together. June joined the club at roughly the same time as Audrey and as beginners they often played golf together. We had also had some enjoyable days playing in open mixed competitions at other clubs and it seemed quite incredible to me, that both my wife and my son were now in the position of having to justify themselves against such rubbish at separate inquisition sessions chaired by the same couple.

As for Revitt's complaint that Ricky had refused to play golf with him; Ricky said this was definitely not true. He had not even spoken to Revitt on the day in question. John Standrin had conducted the draw on the day referred to and John's statement also confirmed that as far as he was aware there had been no incident. Ricky added that he could not understand why the Captain had made the complaint. Don't worry Ricky neither could anyone else apart from Revitt himself and the committee of course since they had decided to indulge Revitt by proceeding with these pathetic complaints.

Most of the meeting inevitably concentrated on the whitewash allegation. Ricky said that in his opinion his mother was being bullied by the Captain, who should not have accused her of acting disgracefully, when in fact she had made a reasonable suggestion to try and avoid an awkward situation. Ricky did not argue with what he had said but stated that under normal circumstances he would have kept his opinions to himself and that he was simply defending his mother. This was supported by letters from Alan Bray and Richard Lomas, who had both been present at the time and had witnessed the whole incident.

Lomas wrote: *"I feel that Ricky was joining in the discussion expressing his opinion on a matter that he is emotionally involved and that this was a spur of the moment comment brought on by the topic of conversation".*

Bray confirmed *"it was at this point that Ricky made his only contribution to the exchange by saying 'you should know Gary, you helped to whitewash the incident'. This was probably an ill-considered remark but it has to be taken in context of an incident where Ricky's mother was being openly criticised in public.*

*The incident ended with Gary remarking that June had embarrassed both Richard Lomas and me. I have to concede that it was indeed embarrassing to see these differences aired in public when it could all have been avoided by respecting June's wishes to play quietly at the back of the field with her son Ricky."*

Perhaps it was time for Mr Revitt to take another look at the Captain's rule book and *"in the event of petty differences try to keep an open mind when expressing an opinion".*

Ricky was asked by Pigott if on reflection he regretted his actions. He promptly replied he had no regrets in defending his mother and that any criticism of his actions should also apply to the Captain. In theory Ricky that was a very practical and sensible thing to say, in practice however it was not going to happen.

For myself, I would just like to add that I am proud of the way Ricky conducted himself in the face of such obvious discrimination by the Captain. The disgrace in my eyes is that the committee indulged Revitt by going along with his unfair and clearly prejudicial treatment of my family. Brian Shaw by the way, despite his former concerns, said nothing at all at the meeting on Ricky's behalf.

It was another six weeks before Pigott responded to Ricky with the Management Committee's decision. It arrived on 31st January 2003, the same day the committee had finally decided to hold the EGM to have my expulsion ratified by the members.

Ricky was warned not to disrupt the 'ambience or harmony' of the club again. He was also instructed not to disagree or the committee would reconvene and consider their options. In other words Ricky - don't speak, or breathe, or give an opinion on any subject; don't even look at anyone in the wrong way or you will be out. To satisfy the committee's requirements Ricky would have to sit in silence wearing blinkers, fearing his every movement or utterance (no matter how innocent) was being monitored. Revitt in particular and the committee in general had accomplished what they set out to do. No other member of the Club would have been subjected to such an ordeal based on such complete drivel and any unbiased committee would have reprimanded Revitt for abusing his position.

Even worse tactics meanwhile were being applied to June. Her treatment at the hands of the committee bordered on the despicable. You may recall that the Ladies Committee had sent their findings of Mrs Revitt's complaint to the Management Committee but June had not been informed of their decision and was still awaiting official notification of the outcome. The committee's 'think tank' meanwhile had not wasted a moment of that time.

On December 5th Thomas Pigott, on behalf of the Management Committee, wrote a letter to June that I think has to be read to be believed.

*"Dear Mrs June Baker,*

*The Management Committee have instructed me to*

177

*inform you that at a Management Meeting on 2nd December 2002, the Management Committee discussed the Ladies Committee's recommendation with regards to the incident on the ladies 11th tee on Saturday 28th September 2002 between Mrs Jean Revitt and yourself.*

*The Ladies Committee's recommendation after interviewing Mrs Jean Revitt and yourself is, as there are no witnesses to the pertinent alleged conversation between Mrs Jean Revitt and Mrs June Baker on the ladies 11th tee, that the matter should now be closed.*

*However, the Management Committee considers that in any situation when it is one person's word against another where there can be no definite proof, a decision may still have to be made. Any decision should be based on balance of probabilities, the surrounding circumstances and taking into account any antecedents".*

Even by the dictionary swallowing Pigott's standards this little paragraph broke new ground. I must admit I had to read it several times before I could actually believe anyone could have the audacity to write it. Perish the thought that Pigott was saying (which of course he was,) that in his humble capacity as servant of the committee of course, my wife must be guilty simply because she happened to be June Baker. If your name was Jean Revitt then that was fine. The letter continued:

*"Therefore the Management Committee before making a final decision, has instructed three*

*members of the Management Committee to form a sub-committee <u>to establish that a fair and thorough investigation has been carried out and any areas of doubt be resolved by interviewing individuals concerned".</u>*

Which individuals for crying out loud? There were no individuals other than June and Mrs Revitt. They had already been interviewed and the recommendation by the Ladies Committee clearly stated <u>*"as there are no witnesses the matter should now be closed".*</u> There could be no areas of doubt. In fact everything was becoming crystal clear; June had to be guilty of something the big shots at Hillsborough had already decided.

This epitomised to me the profound depths to which this committee were prepared to sink in their single minded and cruel determination to victimise and persecute my family. It was yet another shameful example of abuse of power. They wanted rid of us all, that was clear and I was becoming more disgusted by the minute. If this travesty of justice didn't contravene the much threatened 'Article 16' then I don't know what did. In my humble opinion the Committee Members of HGC responsible for this outrage should take heed of the advice they had given to me and **<u>"do the honourable thing and resign!"</u>**

The Management now intended to organise yet another 'interrogation committee'. For over a year I couldn't get them to hold one and now you couldn't stop them.

Had they nothing better to do than continually harass

my family. How many interrogations did it take to establish that a disagreement between two people was just that! It could not be proved or disproved when and forgive me for repeating this **'there were no witnesses'.** The ladies had had words on the golf course: there was no physical contact, no-one was attacked or threatened, unlike other incidents I could mention. Any normal person in a civilised society would consider that to be the end of the story but not at Hillsborough, where the committee as we know are a law unto themselves. Only in a regime like this would anyone persist in such circumstances.

If every Hillsborough Golf Club member were persecuted like this there would be no members and there would be no club.

How arrogant they were to suggest that the recommendation by the Ladies Committee wasn't satisfactory or thorough simply because the outcome wasn't acceptable to them. In my experience any insight the Management Committee had into conducting fair and thorough investigations could fit into a specimen jar and there would still be room to spare. When it came to serious complaints involving their own upper circle the committee were seasoned experts in avoiding them. The complaint against June should never have gone ahead. Eric Liddell had said as much after speaking to Pigott on the day of the incident, Eric thought that would be an end to the matter. This was pure victimisation.

For weeks June had awaited official confirmation that the matter of Mrs Revitt's complaint was now closed. What other verdict could there possibly be? Pigott was not finished yet however;

*"Other incidents, concerning your behaviour have been reported to the Management Committee. These may be taken into consideration, in particular incidents, which have occurred on the first tee and around the clubhouse. The Management Committee will be considering statements from members who witnessed the above incident".*

Was this another form of mental torture and what could this possibly have to do with the complaint June had already answered.

*"If the sub-committee finds that there is a case to answer then a disciplinary committee made up of the officers who carried out the initial investigation will hold a disciplinary hearing where the member will be given adequate notice of the time and place of the hearing, and given the opportunity to contend and contest the allegation. The member will also have the right to be accompanied by a fellow member or make a written submission.*

*Having satisfied themselves that they have all the evidence they will then report to the Management Committee their findings and a decision will be made.*

*Once this investigation is complete you will of course be fully informed of their findings and have an opportunity to respond."*

How very kind! Presumably by this time Pigott will have decided what other incident(s) have been reported.

Had Pigott swallowed a law book along with the dictionary? Where was all this bureaucratic rigmarole going on in the serious misconduct of Timms whose wrongdoing was irrefutable and what of Captain Hall's antics? He too was let off scot-free, with his place on committee still intact and he was now party to this particularly nasty and vicious persecution of a woman simply because she happened to be my wife.

Pigott, who by now had built up a good head of steam, was still not finished; making good use of the committee's nice little bylaw passed on October 21st he closed his letter with one of the most spiteful things he had ever written to a member of the Baker family. In fact it was the most spiteful, written by a man at the bidding of an all male Club Committee, who would not dare discipline any of their own, despite knowing of their misconduct but could do this to a woman who had done absolutely nothing wrong. The punch line read:

*"Meanwhile, in the club's and your best interest, your membership is being suspended from receipt of this letter until 23rd December 2002. If the sub-committee find no case to answer, then the suspension will be lifted immediately. However, if the sub-committee do find a case to answer the suspension will continue until a full Management Committee reaches a decision. (By-laws relating to suspension of membership are displayed on the Club House notice board".)*

*Yours sincerely*

*Thomas C. Pigott*
*Hon. Secretary*

June had turned decidedly pale, she was devastated. Even I, who had become an expert on the breathtaking audacity of the Management Committee at Hillsborough, could not believe the cruelty and arrogance that they had shown here. Who could possibly justify drafting such a despicable letter? June had been a club member for 14 years and had supported the club and the ladies section without a blemish on her character. She had declined for personal reasons when approached to consider the position of Lady Captain but had assisted with the job of handicap secretary and represented the ladies 'A' team in their inter-club league team matches. She also now held the dubious honour of being the first lady member ever to be suspended from Hillsborough Golf Club.

It seems you can be persecuted, suspended or even expelled and you are not entitled to an independent appeal. In fact you are not entitled to any appeal. The matter is always closed and the committee will not enter into any further correspondence. There is no regard for the law of Natural Justice where everyone is treated equal and is innocent until proved guilty, Pigott's letter was evidence of that.

After a few days, which quite frankly June needed to take stock of the situation, she wrote back expressing her shock and bewilderment at the committee's decision to ignore the ladies' findings and to suspend her membership.

June asked if the same procedures were being applied to the Captain's wife. This seemed reasonable, since in the case of Mrs Revitt the committee didn't need a crystal ball. Her outburst had been witnessed by the other three. No need for probabilities, surrounding circumstances, antecedents or any of that rubbish. It was also suggested that Pigott might like to explain why any suspension could be in June's best interest. Not only would everyone at the golf club know about it and obviously assume the worst but having lived for the past 30 years barely a mile from the course, the local community would also be aware of it. June requested confirmation that Mrs Revitt's membership had also been suspended. If as Pigott suggested this was in June's best interest then surely the same applied to the Captain's wife.

In addition if there was some other complaint, June asked to be informed of the details. (She had to assume that this latest incident referred to the episode with Hall and Revitt over two months earlier.) If so, then why had Pigott not made this clear? He had already had the witness statements relating to this incident for at least three weeks in connection with the same complaint against Ricky. That was more than enough time for the committee to have studied them. This pretext of making investigations was just a ploy, nothing more than an excuse to make use of their new bylaw to suspend and discredit June.

Just as in 2001, Christmas 2002 in the Baker household was dominated by the shenanigans of the Golf Club. It was now the last day of June's suspension from the club and if by chance she may have been planning to join in the festive activities with the other lady members, Mr Pigott decided to deliver his personal message of glad tidings and he rang June at home. This extra little treat took place on Sunday 22nd December just as we were on our way out of the door to join in a family Christmas lunch at June's sister's house.

Pigott kindly informed June that she should not visit the golf club premises as the suspension imposed on her by the committee had been extended pending further enquiries and he wanted to be sure she got the message in advance of a letter which he had written to her that same day.

You have to give Pigott his due, he certainly was dedicated to the cause; writing letters and making phone calls on a Sunday, just a couple of days prior to Christmas. One could almost be forgiven for thinking he actually enjoyed it. Sadly his phone call did absolutely nothing to help June's state of mind as you may well imagine, in fact he managed to completely ruin what had promised to be an enjoyable family gathering. Well done Pigott; how might you feel if I telephoned your home in similar circumstances.

The effect all this was having on June's health was becoming clear. She had lost over a stone in weight and barely tipped the seven stone marker on the scales. We both suffered from insomnia and dreaded the arrival each morning of the mail. June was now in a similar position to the one I had faced. She had done nothing wrong and refused to be pressured into resigning from the Club even though it was clear that was what they wanted.

Confirmation was never received that Jean Revitt had been suspended, which came as no great surprise to either June or myself. On Christmas Eve though, June did receive Thomas Pigott's promised letter written in his best Christmas spirit, confirming that her suspension would continue until the sub-committee had reported to the Management Committee and so on and so forth. The 'other incident' that demanded her continued suspension was finally revealed to be the 5th October fiasco on the first tee, where June was branded disgraceful by the Captain for having made a perfectly sensible suggestion in order to avoid confrontation and which Ricky for his part had already answered.

The specific allegations Revitt made against June were:

1. Where you are alleged to have refused to play in a game of golf with the Captain and Mr. John Hall.

2. You made verbal allegations with regards to the investigation of another member. (The member of course being John Hall, who the Committee were still reluctant to name.)

The incident had occurred on 5th October and this was the first time June had seen the allegations. <u>The complaints had been held in cold storage as it were for over 11 weeks, during which time the Committee had been busy passing the new bylaw, giving themselves the authority to suspend a member pending investigation of any complaint. They had promptly made use of the bylaw by suspending June, although the complaints against her had already taken place well before the bylaw had been proposed.</u>

June had already answered Mrs Revitt's complaint with the Ladies Committee (as club rules require.)

According to the Complaint Procedures June should now attend another meeting with them to answer these further allegations made by the Captain but the Management Committee, not satisfied with the ladies' past findings, decided to dispense with the rules altogether and deal with Mr Revitt's complaints themselves.

According to Pigott this was 'in order to deal with matters as swiftly as possible' (the previous 11 weeks delay had evidently slipped his mind.) Pigott even had the audacity to add that this was in June's best interest.

Pigott also decided to point out that _"the Management Committee have full authority and responsibility for the ambience between members"._ That being the case, it seemed quite characteristic of the committee that they didn't decide to enforce this authority on either Captain Revitt or his predecessor Hall, who obviously assumed (rightly as it happens) that it didn't apply to them. What did the rules matter anyway? The committee could make them or they could break them just as they saw fit. You somehow ended up trying to defend yourself from some ridiculous charge even though you had done nothing wrong in the first place.

June wrote to Pigott. She pointed out that as the latest complaints had been made by a member of the Management Committee, she felt it would be in her own interest if the Club's Procedures were followed. In other words she should answer the complaint as before with the Ladies Committee. It was unlikely they would conform to their own rules, as doing so would allow the Ladies Committee access to witness statements that could prove embarrassing to the Management

Committee. I have copied below the full letter sent to Pigott by club member Mr Alan Bray, who had written in connection with Revitt's allegations:

*"Dear Mr. Pigott*

*I did indeed witness the unfortunate incident on the first tee on the 5th October 2002 when there was an altercation between the Club Captain, Gary Revitt and both Ricky and June Baker.*

*By way of background, I am part of a group which tends to play at the same time on Saturday's throughout the season. Before recent unfortunate events the group also included Roger, June and Ricky Baker, together with Gary Revitt and John Hall.*

*The well publicised dispute between Roger Baker and the Club Committee, and the subsequent incident when John Hall allegedly confronted and threatened Roger Baker in the Clubhouse created some tension within the group and in previous weeks neither Gary Revitt nor John had joined the fiddle.*

*The incident in question occurred shortly after Roger Baker was asked to leave the Club and possibly only a week after a mixed foursomes match involving Gary and June on opposite teams. This clearly presented a difficult situation given the ongoing dispute between June's husband and the Committee of which Gary was a member.*

*On Saturday 5th October a few of the usual group had congregated on the first tee when Gary and John Hall arrived, clearly intending to re-join the fiddle. When Phil Yeardley collected the balls to select the playing partners June quietly informed him that she and Ricky would play together at the back of the field, ostensibly to avoid any embarrassment. Gary took exception to this and confronted her saying that "her behaviour was disgraceful" and "she was seeking to impose her prejudices on others". June responded by asking Gary whether "he really expected her to play golf with a man who had confronted and threatened to assault her husband and no punishment had been imposed by the Club?" It was at this point that Ricky made his only contribution to the exchange by saying "you should know Gary, you helped to whitewash the incident". This was probably an ill considered remark but it has to be taken in context of an incident where Ricky's mother was being openly criticised in public.*

*The incident ended with Gary remarking that June had embarrassed both Richard Lomas and me. I have to concede that it was indeed embarrassing to see these differences aired in public when it could all have been avoided by respecting June's wishes to play quietly at the back of the field with her son Ricky.*

*I have no wish to sit in judgement on any of the individuals who were involved in the incident but I have attempted to give an accurate account of what took place. I trust this will assist the Committee in its deliberations.*

*Yours sincerely*
*Alan Bray"*

Mr Bray had no axe to grind. No back scratching to be gained. He had delivered his account of what happened as it happened. After reading Bray's letter why didn't the committee ask Mr Revitt to account for his behaviour instead of suspending June? The Captain accused June of behaving disgracefully. He caused an embarrassing scene in front of other members, when the incident could have easily been avoided as Mr Bray confirmed. I believe it is revealed throughout this story that Officers of the Club are not held accountable for their conduct no matter how badly they behave.

The Ladies Committee may be surprised to learn how the Club Captain had spoken to June in front of her son and other club members and for what reason had the Management Committee (despite the absence of any witness to Mrs Revitt's complaint,) disregarded the Ladies recommendation that the matter be closed, deciding instead to suspend June from the Club, whilst taking no action at all against Mrs Revitt?

Bray had been asked for his account but because it didn't fit with the committee's own preconceptions, as with the ladies findings, it was simply dismissed.

Before we press on with this sorry saga and Pigott was a slave to firing off missives in between Christmas and the New Year, I would also like to quote another letter sent to the committee by Sheila Hattersley. Now Sheila is a nice person and I have quoted her letter below since once she found out about June's suspension she very kindly took the time over the Christmas period to write the following:

*"I would like to give my account of an incident that happened in the main golfing season earlier this year concerning Mrs June Baker and myself.*

*It took place with Mrs Jean Revitt and Mrs Jean
Willers with regards to arranging a knockout match
in an official ladies club competition. I approached
the ladies named above after playing a Captains' fun
competition to try to arrange a date that was
convenient for all involved.*

*Their reply was we have nothing against you
Sheila but with all the trouble that has happened
recently we don't feel that we could play with June so
we will give you the match.*

*In normal circumstances this would have been the
end of the story however I feel that it now needs
bringing to someone's attention. I fail to see the
difference between the allegation that Mrs Baker
refused to play with the Captain and the reality of
the above, especially as one of the ladies involved
was the Captain's wife"*

Now would the committee take account of this letter?
Well I will let you have one guess; it was treated with the
same disdain as Mr Bray's letter. Sheila was not even
given the courtesy of a reply. I expect you realise by now
that this is standard club practice concerning any
correspondence from members in support of the Baker
family.

Meanwhile Pigott had still been busy firing letters at
the Baker clan. Not only was correspondence received
June had spoken to the man himself, in fact he wrote:

*"I have contacted you by telephone and allowed
you, on this occasion, to contact me by telephone
and fax in order to assist in arranging a meeting as
soon as possible".*

June made one final request for a meeting with the Ladies Committee but this was ignored and sent straight to the Management Committee. June was left with no alternative but to attend a meeting on 13th January 2003. Failure to attend (as with Ricky) was to result in the meeting proceeding in her absence. June wrote back in disgust. She wanted to put on record that she was not guilty of any wrongdoing and could not understand why she had been suspended. Once again June made clear her position in relation to the complaints having been made by a member of the same committee, who (contrary to Club Rules) were also insisting on investigating the complaints.

June's points were possibly a bit too near the truth for the committee's liking as Pigott didn't bother to reply. It's ironic really, after months of dreading letters arriving, when June actually did want a response from the Club none was forthcoming and she reluctantly attended the Meeting as instructed. Attending on behalf of the committee was the President, Bruce Oakes and putting in another appearance was Brian Shaw and of course Thomas Pigott, who was also chairing the meeting. Peter Gleadall, having already supported Ricky, willingly offered to attend with June. The office where the meeting was held was rather small and cramped and there was no table or available space where June or Peter could put their paperwork or make notes. Peter in fact chose to stand rather than balance everything on his knee. I don't expect he anticipated he would still be there three hours later.

In answer to June's previous enquiry, Pigott had indicated that the meeting was not to be taped but at the start of the meeting he suddenly produced a recording machine and after receiving his assurance that a copy of the tape would be provided to them, Peter and June gave their permission for the meeting to be recorded.

June pointed out that in just 17 days from the date I was expelled, the Club Captain, Garry Revitt and his wife had made no less than six complaints in total against her and Ricky. She considered this indicated that the Captain had some sort of a grudge against them but the President, Bruce Oakes disagreed.

June asked what decision the committee had reached concerning Mrs Revitt's complaint. Other than the fact that June's membership was suspended and Mrs Revitt's was not, she did not have the slightest clue what was happening. Pigott said this meeting was not to discuss that incident and refused to comment but June persisted. She said that Mrs Revitt's allegation had now been hanging over her for well over three months. Pigott finally conceded that no decision had yet been reached.

It was quite unbelievable; a squabble on the golf course with no witnesses, yet three months later (despite throwing out the Ladies' recommendation that the matter should be dropped) the Management Committee had still not reached a decision. Don't rush chaps – wouldn't want to be hasty and arrive at the wrong conclusion. What a pity the decision to suspend June didn't receive this much consideration; I suppose it was fortunate she was not charged with attacking someone in the dining room or she could still be under suspension next Christmas.

As for the Captain's allegation that June had refused to play in a game of golf with him and John Hall, June said she had not refused to play golf with the Captain but she would not have been willing to play golf with John Hall under any circumstances and both the Captain and Hall knew this when they arrived on the tee. The whole incident had already been explained and substantiated in statements from Mr Lomas and Mr Bray who had been present at the time but June again confirmed the same facts.

Peter Gleadall said he could quote endless instances where members chose not to play golf with people they didn't get along with, it happened all the time. This was simply a question of personalities and was accepted. Peter said he had conducted numerous draws in his time and quoted a particular instance where he had already drawn for partners and an ex. Captain refused to play with his drawn partner and it had to be re-drawn. Peter had been a member of Hillsborough for well over thirty years and never in his experience had anyone ever been reported or disciplined let alone suspended for this reason.

June raised the question posed by Miss Hattersley, who had written to the Club regarding Mrs Revitt's refusal to play golf with June in an official club competition. According to the President, this had been denied by Mrs Revitt, who alleged it was her partner Mrs Willers who had refused. That was quite alright then, Miss Hattersley must of course be wrong if Mrs Revitt said so. We already know her word cannot be disputed and this explanation seemed to satisfy Bruce Oakes. The fact she had pointed the finger at Mrs Willers evidently didn't bother Oakes as he saw no problem with her refusal to play either. No chance of this charge being pursued against anyone else then. It seemed everything the Revitt's said was taken at face value. What a feeling it must be, to be in such a privileged position. June's word on the other hand wouldn't be accepted no matter how much evidence there was to back it up. It was extremely exhausting to continually keep fighting an uphill battle.

As for the Captain's second complaint, June said she had not made any allegation about the investigation into John Hall; she had simply said 'you can't expect me to play golf with a man who threatened to assault my husband in the club dining room and no action was taken.' This also was confirmed in Lomas and Bray's statements. It was not an allegation she said but simply a statement of fact.

June had given her account of what happened on the first tee but it really didn't matter that she had done nothing wrong; the damage had already been done and she had been severely punished anyway. The fact that she had been suspended had obviously given credence to the offensive rumours, which she had been given no opportunity to dispel. Mrs Revitt on the other hand had continued as normal, playing golf and visiting the club as usual in her role as the Captain's wife. June said that due to her prolonged suspension everyone would assume she was guilty. Oakes merely shrugged his shoulders.

The President Bruce Oakes did however offer up one pearl of wisdom;

Peter Gleadall asked who attended the meeting where it was voted to suspend June.

There had been only one absentee and Oakes confirmed that both Garry Revitt and John Hall had taken part and voted at the meeting. This meeting you may recall was where the committee had discussed Mrs Revitt's complaint against June and rejected the Ladies' findings (that as there were no witnesses the matter should be closed) and voted instead to suspend June's membership, whilst deciding to take no action at all against Mrs Revitt. Oakes even blatantly added that he saw nothing wrong in Hall and Revitt's participation in the meeting.

He completely rejected June's claim that Revitt's presence must have created a total conflict of interest.

Peter Gleadall said Revitt should not have voted and should also have excused himself from the meeting.

Revitt and Hall also voted on the new bylaw which resulted in the committee suspending June in the first place. In fact the pair of them were not excluded from any of the Meetings where June and Mrs Revitt were discussed. They were even in on the Meeting where Revitt's own complaints of June were dealt with; despite the fact both Revitt and Hall had been directly involved in the incident.

June was completely overwhelmed. She said she couldn't see how Revitt could possibly be impartial when he and his wife had made the allegations. It was farcical that the committee even considered Revitt to be a fair person to sit in judgement. With Hall and Revitt at the meetings June was immediately two votes down. Revitt's presence must have also created the most embarrassing state of affairs. How could other Committee Members possibly give an honest opinion or cast a fair vote with Revitt hovering over them? They were never going to vote in June's favour against Revitt or his wife no matter what facts were put in front of them. As with the hearing to expel me, it should have been conducted by an independent panel. If there had been any intention at all of dealing with the matters fairly, they would, at the very least, have insisted Revitt exclude himself. It was little wonder that June and Ricky never stood the remotest chance of a fair hearing. June asked why the committee had allowed Revitt to participate in the meetings. The smug response came from Bruce Oakes *"He is the Captain"*.

Particularly in light of the above facts, June asked why (contrary to the Club's Rules of Procedure) her requests to answer Garry Revitt's complaints before the Ladies Committee had been refused. Pigott actually had the effrontery to say that he had written the rules covering the Complaints Procedures and was at liberty to change them whenever he wished. What complete arrogance! June pointed out that the rules had not been changed and were therefore still the current Procedures of the Club. Pigott made no comment.

In a letter dated 29th January 2003, the exact same date as Ricky's, Pigott informed June that at the previous evenings Management Committee meeting all the allegations against her had been discussed at length. There was no mention of whether Garry Revitt's wife's antics were also discussed at length, I presume they were not. June's suspension was finally lifted and all matters were deemed closed. In fact he repeated word for word what he had written to Ricky.

*"The Management Committee have instructed me to inform you that after discussing alleged actions against you at length they came to the following conclusion.*

*The Management Committee regards your conduct with regards to these incidents has not been in the best interest of the Club as a whole.*

*It should be noted that the Management Committee will not ignore or condone any disrespect to officials of the club or incidents where any member disrupts the ambience and harmony of the club".*

It went on to say that there should be no recurrence of June's actions and should she disagree with the Management Committee they would reconvene and consider their options. Well that told you June. I am sure that by now you will also realise that they told Jean Revitt absolutely nothing. Garry Revitt continued his term as Captain and June has not spoken to either him or his wife since.

As a footnote to this little scenario, despite giving his assurance at the start of the meeting that June would receive a copy of the tape, Pigott has since decided that June could not have one.

She in fact made six written requests for a copy. Initially his reason was that the tape was of 'poor quality', now she cannot have one because 'the matter is closed and the committee are not prepared to enter into any further correspondence.' Her final requests were simply ignored.

One little anecdote may shed some light on my feelings of despair at the part played in this latest saga by committee man John Hall. It was during the early stages of my dispute with the club and it was John Hall's Captain's Day. Both my brothers and their wives and June and I had attended. John's mother-in-law had recently passed away and his wife Christine, who had been very close to her mother, was naturally upset. June literally spent hours sifting through hundreds of old photographs and negatives to find the one single picture she had of John and Christine, with Christine's mother taken in happier times. June arranged for the photograph to be enlarged and framed and gave it to Christine in private later that day. Christine was very emotional and said it was the most thoughtful gift she had ever been given. John very kindly repeated these sentiments in his speech. When I think back on this and other past occasions it makes the disgrace of what happened to my wife and to my son all the more painful.

After what he has been through Ricky quite frankly feels demoralised. He knows he is spot the ball and simply cannot be himself anymore. The politics and backstabbing at Hillsborough Golf Club have left him disillusioned with the whole place. He has all but given up the sport he loves and rarely visits the club anymore. So well done chaps, mission definitely accomplished. You should be thoroughly ashamed.

June is pretty much in the same position. She still plays golf occasionally with friends but not nearly as often as she used to. She has lost the interest and enthusiasm she had when we both played and still she has to face the indignity of walking up and down the long drive from the main road like some outcast. Many members have been extremely kind but no-one knows the true story of why she was suspended or the injustices she and Ricky were made to suffer.

During that 2002 season June was also Lady Golfer of the Year. She was still under suspension however. The prize giving took place on 14th January 2003, at the Ladies AGM. June wasn't permitted to attend and her prize was kindly collected by one of the other lady members in her absence. She was I thought treated ever so well. I guess the congratulatory letter from Thomas Pigott 'on behalf of the Management Committee' is still in the post.

Later that year June suffered health problems resulting in a mild heart attack. Thankfully her condition, attributed mainly to stress, appears with the proper medication to be under control. I have seen at first hand the terrible heartache June and Ricky have had to endure and there is no doubt in my mind that the hurtful and cruel victimisation of my son and especially my wife contributed to what happened.

# Chapter 10

# One Member One Vote

So I had been expelled from the club. Thomas Pigott at
the bidding of the Management Committee had told me
so and they intended to hold an EGM as soon as possible
to have their verdict ratified by the members. I have to
admit I couldn't quite see the point of that when the
decision to expel me had already been taken and
implemented. The odd thing was the committee had
stated that their ruling was final and no matter which
way the members voted they were not prepared to
reinstate my membership. Unless I was missing
something here I appeared to be in a no win situation.

I had declined to attend the meeting where I was
expelled. My solicitor and I agreed it was pointless
trying to defend myself when the ones sitting in
judgement were also my accusers; they had made the
charges so it was inevitable I would be found guilty and
in their consistently undemocratic fashion, they had
refused to allow my solicitor to act in my defence. We
have all heard the phrase judge and jury but the
committee had taken on the role of prosecutor as well.
Those responsible for covering up for Timms had
decided I was guilty of conduct injurious to the Club and
they were running the show so it was impossible to
argue. The outcome had obviously been a foregone
conclusion but I did make two requests.

1. I asked that the committee's decision to expel me
   should not take effect until after members had

voted at the EGM, as doing so was likely to pre-judge the outcome of that meeting. It was the committee's choice to have their decision endorsed by the members, so it would at least seem fair to wait for the result of the voting before passing judgement. Once the committee's decision to expel me had already been made and implemented, it seemed less likely that the members would vote to overturn it.

2. Due to the special nature of the EGM, I also requested that Proxy Votes should not be allowed.

The committee refused on both counts.

My objection to the use of Proxy Votes was twofold:

It had always been customary that any member wishing to vote by proxy was required to make a personal application for the form at the Secretary's Office, returning it to him 48 hours prior to the meeting. (The director's report produced annually still states this.) Only the serious voter had been likely to take the trouble.

You will recall however, that on the occasion of the EGM to discuss the sale of land, the committee decided to make some changes and in order to ensure the maximum number of proxy votes were returned, they sent out voting forms, accompanied by a return stamped addressed envelope to every member. You may also recall that the wording of the form ensures that in the absence of a specified nominee, all returned proxy votes are allocated to the President. You can see the massive impact this could have on the overall vote. Hillsborough is traditionally noted for having a low attendance to General Meetings, so there was every possibility that due to the changes, the number of proxy votes could easily outweigh the numbers attending the meeting.

One other important factor that most members would not be aware of; because of the committee's refusal to delay my expulsion until after the EGM, this meant I would attend the meeting as an ex-member and as such any proxy votes allocated to me personally would therefore be invalid and not included in the vote. Nice touch! As the only resolution to be voted on was my expulsion, the only fair way in my view would be to put the resolution on the voting form itself; in that way the members would at least have control over which way their vote was cast but fair was not a word the committee set much store by. You had to hand it to them; they had every angle covered. It was obvious in the circumstances that the odds were stacked firmly against me. The best I could hope for in the circumstances was to try and get my side across to the members who actually took the trouble to turn up at the meeting. Unfortunately we were unlikely to forget the debacle of the last EGM and the shameful way we were treated. It was not an experience we cared to repeat.

The club were to send to members all the correspondence and a similar copy had already been provided to each committee member prior to their vote on my expulsion. Meanwhile I had been given just two working days in which to check through the stuff. This turned out to be a mammoth task. As you might imagine there was a lot of paperwork to go through and to make matters worse it was not arranged in chronological order or any logical order for that matter, therefore much of it made no sense. I could see the intention was the same as before, to swamp everyone with masses of paperwork, arranged in such a fashion it would be impossible to make sense of.

Even worse from my point of view, when putting the correspondence together 'someone' had decided on what might be described as a 'selective process'; this was to send out loads of documentation, whilst selectively removing numerous letters and statements. This must have been an extremely time consuming exercise and all the missing items, needless to say, supported my side of the case and were crucial if the dispute was to be shown in its true light.

To give an example the following are some of the removed items:

One of the more significant of the 'missing documents' was the confirmation by John Hall that Derek Brown had no reason to make any complaint against me. On the same issue was the solicitor's correspondence to Derek Pinning and Pinning's reply, confirming that he had never witnessed me making any derogatory remarks to Derek Brown. Also gone were the letters Pinning had written, requesting an explanation of the allegation against me and the correspondence from the club's solicitor, stating that 'Derek Brown was unhappy for his letter to be released'. Nowhere to be seen either was the letter confirming that Garry Revitt had witnessed the over my dead body remark made by Jack Timms to the other bidder or the statements given by Henry Barber and Bob Turnbull that all bids for the

Stubbing Lane land would be posted on the notice board. Several key letters from my solicitor requesting answers to extremely significant questions were also missing. One such letter made particular reference to John Hall's visit to my house with the suggestion that if I were to drop my complaint against Timms, all reference to my appearance before the committee would then be deleted from the minutes. My letter offering a without prejudice meeting be held in an attempt to reach some common ground had also made it to the cutting room floor. Probably most significant of all was the absence of the entire correspondence in connection with the sale of land at Stubbing Lane. I think by now you get the picture. Of course this also meant the same letters and statements were excluded from the information provided to the full committee who voted on my expulsion.

I have already used the word 'selective' to describe the correspondence going out to the members; I should have prefixed it with the word 'extremely'.

Following my letter of complaint some of the removed letters were later replaced but these were put at the very back where they made no logical sense. The Stubbing Lane letters were not sent out at all. In fact a great deal of time and effort had gone into all this removing and re-arranging in order to paint a completely different picture of the dispute, or at least the part played by the committee. Who was responsible for this?

Whilst this magic act of disappearing correspondence was taking place another conundrum occurred. Other communications had been conjured up from nowhere and were now included as part of the original correspondence. These were in fact what can only be described as 'internal memos' written by Timms and certain other committee members to themselves, recounting their 'recollections' of what had taken place at the disciplinary meeting I had attended. The reason I say written to themselves was because they had never previously been seen by me, my solicitor or anyone else for that matter and had apparently been put together over one year after the infamous meeting and were now magically being pulled out of the hat. I may not know much about the goings on in committees but even I, with my limited knowledge, understood that it was the minutes that were a record of a meeting, not the belated ramblings of individuals trying to cover up for obvious wrongdoings. If these 'recollections' had any relevance at all, why had they not been produced during the course of our long dispute? Nevertheless I'm sure this fiction made much more interesting bedside reading for the members than the real correspondence which had been removed.

It was based on this total misrepresentation of the facts that the full committee had voted to expel me. If there had been nothing to hide why resort to such measures?

I sometimes wondered if certain matters were left in the hands of the more prominent committee members. I must confess, I found it difficult to understand how people I had never had a problem with could be party to all that had happened, especially concerning June and Ricky, whose dreadful treatment, based on the most petty and ridiculous charges was unforgivable. I could hardly believe that anyone could justify such actions. It was also a noticeable fact how more or less the same select few seemed to take charge of disciplinary matters.

Meanwhile we had requested a copy of the Captain's letter which apparently was to be sent to all members. It was such a nice letter I have quoted it here in its entirety.

*"Fellow member*

*As Captain of our club, I would like to make you aware of my own feelings regarding the forthcoming EGM.*

*I can assure all members that the resolution being put before you, has come as a last resort and is being taken with great regret.*

*Since I joined the committee in March 2001, there have been very few Management Committee meetings which did not have Mr. Roger Baker as an item on the agenda.*

*The committee and immediate past captain, Mr. John Hall, have attempted on numerous occasions to bring the matter to an amicable conclusion: but without success.*

*My main concern is the disharmony that this has caused within the club, Mr. Roger Baker now chooses to totally ignore myself and the other officers of the club and he continues to be a disruptive influence within the club.*

*A few weeks ago on the first tee, I was saddened to witness Mr. Roger Baker imposing his own prejudices on his fellow members by refusing to play with Mr. John Hall, should they have been drawn to play together in the fiddle they have played in for years.*

*This is our golf club, a place for recreation and friendship. We must not allow anyone to use it to pursue personal arguments.*

*It is for this reason that I urge you to support this resolution."*

*Garry Revitt*
*Captain*

Revitt seemed to have forgotten that his actual purpose as Captain was to inform the members about the EGM and encourage them to attend. In other words he was supposed to try and be neutral. Revitt on the other hand had decided to take another path and was espousing the cause of his beloved committee. He seemed determined to tell the rest of the membership what jolly good chaps they were and what a nasty piece of work I was. It was complete drivel written by a man who couldn't grasp a daffodil let alone a nettle.

Whilst creating this literary masterpiece however, Mr Revitt does appear to have been somewhat economical with the truth, or had it completely slipped his mind that Hall's idea of *"an amicable conclusion"* was to attempt to assault me across the dining table? I was physically threatened by a lifelong friend and at the risk of banging my drum too much it was the illustrious Captain who hushed it up, yet here he was telling members *"this is our golf club, a place for recreation and friendship. We must not allow anyone to use it to pursue personal arguments."* Surely it would have been more appropriate to address this little sermon to his friend Hall. Would

Revitt have taken such a benevolent attitude I wonder if I had attacked him in front of his wife and family? For someone who had already proved to be of such a sensitive disposition, I very much doubt it.

Taking account of Hall's conduct and Revitt's own treatment of my wife and son, what right did he have to preach such sanctimonious rubbish? It was obviously just a premeditated attempt to influence the membership. Of course the majority of members reading the Captain's letter had no idea what a complete hypocrite the writer was.

Garry Revitt with his selective grasp of disciplinary matters was telling the membership as a whole, that all you jolly committee members in general and John Hall in particular, were just trying to bring everything to an amicable conclusion. Revitt seemed to have overlooked the fact that all matters had been concluded until Timms/Turnbull/Hall & Co decided to re-open them with the recent fiasco of the public notice. As for choosing to ignore you and these other fine 'Officers', what would we talk about Garry, your refusal to discipline other committee members or possibly your neurosis at being looked at? Perhaps the latest swear words used by lady golfers? I am sure the list is endless but I don't think they would have made the most sparkling of conversations. Apparently I was imposing my prejudices on members yet it never seemed to enter Revitt's head that here he was imposing his own.

Notification of the missing documentation meanwhile had been advised to the Club a few days after my expulsion on 18th September 2002. The EGM to ratify my expulsion was supposed to take place as soon as possible afterwards but this in fact dragged on and on and finally took place on the last day of January the following year, by which time whatever sympathy or support I may have got from members at the time of my expulsion had long since evaporated. Basically the meeting was now to be held shortly before the AGM, making any consideration of a vote of no confidence in the committee seem pretty pointless to the members.

Extracts of a letter sent by my solicitor just about sums up the situation:

*"Yet again, this therefore serves only to suggest that the intent of the committee is to have Mr. Baker expelled by whatever means and that there is little interest in the matter being dealt with in a fair way or in a way which enables the members properly to decide upon the merits of the parties.*

*When our client was called to appear before the Management Committee in September in connection with his proposed expulsion, he decided not to attend because firstly, he did not consider that he would get a fair hearing (the Committee included the people who had complained about our client) and secondly he had received confirmation that the issue of his expulsion would be put to an E.G.M, for consideration by the Members in whom our client has faith. Now, it would appear that the prospect of the Members being able to form a fair view of the issues will be hampered significantly, and to our clients detriment, by the way in which the documentation is being presented."*

Anyway the Management Committee finally fired off the documentation informing all members that I had been expelled. This was the first time the rank and file membership as a whole had actually been made aware of the situation and this was explained to them in a covering letter which I have dissected out of a sense of my own injustice. The letter they sent out to all club members opened with:

*"Over the past two years the Committee has patiently listened to and politely responded to Mr. Roger Baker's grievances"*

In case they hadn't noticed this whole affair began when I was hauled in front of the committee without being given any reason, despite having done nothing to merit such a meeting. I stood accused of making remarks about Jack Timms which neither Timms nor any other committee member could justify at the time and haven't done since. I wouldn't say I had been politely responded to at any time. As for being listened to I can safely say I would not be writing this now if I had been listened to, I would still be playing golf at Hillsborough.

*"This dispute with Mr. Roger Baker has involved two Presidents, three Captains and three Committees"*

This was another piece of creative writing, designed to give members the impression there had been a considerable turnover of Officers and committee members during our dispute but this was not true. Between April 2001, when the club first involved their solicitor, and January 31st 2003 the date of the EGM to ratify my expulsion, not one new member had been elected onto committee by the members. Also the three Captains, Turnbull, Hall and Revitt were all figures central to the dispute and all three still remained on committee.

Oakes was already Vice President to Timms and from day one he has headed the committee which refused to investigate Timms' actions as I requested. Pigott was already on the committee and also took over the role of Secretary, so in effect we have a position which I would consider to be very much a closed shop.

Forgive me if I briefly recap on a few facts about this illustrious group of Presidents and Captains:

If it had not been for Timms, the first of the two Presidents mentioned, none of this would have happened at all. The second President, Bruce Oakes, instead of dealing with my complaint demanded (under threat of expulsion) that I should extend a written apology to Timms.

The actions of the three Captains speak for themselves. Although Brown had already confirmed he had no reason to make any complaint about me, (the then Captain and close friend of Timms) Bob Turnbull, approached Brown and obtained a letter from him contradicting everything he had previously stated; whereas Hall, who confirmed in writing that the allegation Timms made was a tissue of lies, later proposed it should be swept under the carpet.

Practically the first duty assigned to Captain Revitt on succession from his friend John Hall was to see that Hall didn't forfeit his place on the committee, following his skirmish over the club dining table. Having honed his skills at handling complaints, Revitt then progressed to making them with a one man crusade against my wife and son. Revitt then lacked the integrity to excuse himself from the Management Meetings where his own pathetic catalogue of allegations were discussed and voted on.

It is the faces of these people who adorn the clubhouse walls.

The committee's letter continued:

*"The dispute basically covers three issues"*

1. *"The proposed sale of land at Stubbing Lane and subsequent calling of an EGM by Mr. Roger Baker. Which was defeated"*

Well I could not argue about the EGM. It was called by me and over 70 other members, as was our right and yes it was defeated. In fact Bruce Oakes closed the meeting so fast it barely got off the ground and letters like the one written by member Andy Senior were kept well hidden and went unanswered. Would the committee perhaps care to explain to the members what actually did happen with the Potting Shed and the proposed sale of land? On the other hand I guess they were not that keen or they would not have removed it from the correspondence. Above all I fail to understand and would be delighted if the committee could please enlighten me on this point - <u>'on what basis does this constitute a reason for my expulsion?'</u>

An enormous question mark still hangs over the entire proceedings in connection with the land; from the prejudicial handling of the proposed sale, to the enforced demolition of the unauthorised storage building that replaced the original Potting Shed, which was now lost for good. Timms and the committee (or whoever took charge of the matter) did not only hold the Council Planning Authority in contempt, in my opinion they also held the members of Hillsborough Golf Club in contempt. If any matter warranted resignation, this surely must be it.

> 2. *"Remarks by Mr. Roger Baker to a member of the Golf Club inferring some sort of corruption on the construction of the kitchen extension. Which he now denies"*

This was the most blatant misrepresentation of all. Why not tell the members the truth? <u>I did not make any allegation.</u> The written evidence of both John Hall and Derek Pinning support this and the subsequent cover up when Brown was approached to change his story only serves to highlight this.

I never made any derogatory remarks as the evidence confirms and to add *"which he now denies"* is quite simply a bare-faced lie intended to imply to the members that I had previously admitted it. Please check your minutes of that meeting (the ones that you offered to destroy) which categorically state and I quote *"Mr Baker denied he had made any such comments and refuted any allegations made that he had acted against the integrity of Hillsborough Golf Club and its members"*.

This incident may well constitute grounds for expulsion but certainly not mine.

Perhaps as a matter of interest the committee would have been more honest here if they had written: 'Derogatory remarks by Jack Timms to Mr Willers, stating it was his intention to keep Mr Baker out of the bidding for the Stubbing Lane land, of which we do have written evidence that we have chosen to ignore.'

> 3. *"Threats of legal action from him for defamation resulting from past Presidents and Captains suggesting a resolution at the 2002 AGM that he pays legal costs incurred by the Club. The Club has been advised by Counsel that this accusation is unfounded"*

This was a public notice and it was defamatory. They omitted to state here that the proposed resolution also threatened my expulsion under Article 16, if I failed to comply with their demands. They could have simply removed the notice as we requested. Neither did they bother to explain that the committee were finally obliged to back down and withdraw the resolution despite the following letter, written to my solicitor by the President, Bruce Oakes.

> *"The annual general meeting will proceed for the will of the membership to be expressed at that meeting. Mr. Baker is entitled to attend and make such observations as he sees fit; indeed we will be delighted to see Mr. Baker at the meeting."*

I was publicly threatened with expulsion which I had

done nothing to instigate. Whatever issues I had with the committee had been dropped months earlier and I had attempted to get on with my life until matters were again resurrected by the notice. What did they suppose I would do, sit back and wait to be kicked out when I had done nothing wrong? The notice also falsely claimed that the committee had received overwhelming support from the membership. This again was blatant misrepresentation, the first time the membership and I knew of the resolution was when it appeared on the notice board. The statement was clearly designed to brainwash those who read it into going along with the proposed resolution. The committee subsequently disclaimed all knowledge or responsibility for the notice or the resolution, despite the fact that senior members of that committee had taken part in the meeting and it was chaired by the Club President, Bruce Oakes.

This latest action had probably resulted in almost doubling the legal costs they were actually attempting to re-claim (somewhere in the region of £2000 for the club 'or more accurately the members' as well as a similar amount for me.)

These were the three disputes used as a basis for my expulsion. Not one of them was as a result of any wrongdoing on my part. In fact the opposite was the case.

They followed up with what briefly summarised amounted to a character assassination of Mr Roger Baker. I could reply to each point but it is basically a rehash of what has already been covered. Suffice it to say I am disrupting the harmony of the club and as I have refused to remove myself from membership by resigning, as they suggested, the committee courtesy of Article 16 have decided to do it for me.

Why ask for my resignation? If I had accused Timms of corruption as claimed, the committee had the authority and were fully entitled to expel me as they had threatened back in April 2001. Since that time the committee have admittedly spent in total, between £4,000 and £5000 of member's money in legal fees (this does not include an approximate £2,000 for the forthcoming EGM, a meeting to ratify a decision the committee had already taken and implemented.) The truth is I am not the guilty party, I am the victim and to protest Timms' innocence when he was clearly guilty of serious misconduct was depressingly consistent with the policy the committee have repeatedly shown in closing ranks whenever one of their own does something wrong, no matter how badly they have conducted themselves. If anyone has acted against the interests of Hillsborough Golf Club it is Mr Timms and those responsible for what has happened to me initially and more recently to my family.

The evening of the long awaited EGM finally arrived. The question of whether June would be allowed to attend at all had hung in the balance. It wasn't until the actual day of the meeting that both she and Ricky were to receive the Committee's deliberation of the 'charges' against them and it seemed extremely unlikely this was a coincidence. Both were warned not to disrupt the ambience and harmony of the club again and June's suspension was finally lifted. We had not had any contact with the club for quite some time and to return under these circumstances wasn't a prospect any of us looked forward to. If the intention had been to discredit us as a family then I would have to say they had probably done a pretty good job.

I felt a sense of finality and sadness which I couldn't possibly describe. It was especially difficult for June. She had been ostracised for no reason and had no idea of what, or if indeed any explanation had been given for her 'prolonged absence', or had it simply been left to the rumourmongers to spread the good tidings. I felt extremely sorry for both my wife and my son who had done nothing to deserve the treatment they had encountered.

We had arrived and were about to take a seat when I was approached with instructions from Pigott that I was no longer a member of the club and had failed to sign the visitor's book. I was then made to suffer the indignity of being escorted like a criminal back out of the clubhouse in order to fulfil this vital requirement. Along with this final display of authority and arrogance, went any illusion I may have had that this meeting would be any different to the last EGM.

This was endorsed by the attitude of the President, Bruce Oakes. A past Captain Michael Byrne had asked to address the meeting. His concern was in relation to the recent practice which had been adopted in order to obtain inordinate numbers of proxy votes for the use of one member (i.e. The President.) This practice had not happened in the past, Byrne pointed out, so why was it happening now? Byrne quoted the Articles of Association which state *"one member one vote"* and stressed the system was being abused. It was undemocratic and had not been intended that one member should have such power as to possibly decide the outcome of a general meeting. Byrne added that it should be for the members who had turned up to listen to the arguments on both sides to decide Mr Baker's fate and not the President. Oakes however was determined to have me out at all costs and in his usual well thought out manner replied *"what would you have me do, give half the votes to Baker?"* Another member Gerry White stood up and supported Byrne. White maintained, as did Mr Byrne, that the system being used was completely unfair. The Captain, Garry Revitt ended the discussion claiming his own expertise on the subject and there was to be no further debate on the issue.

Another member Dave Green said he had taken the trouble to sort out all the documentation and couldn't see where Roger Baker had done anything wrong and had simply defended himself. Others echoed the same sentiments. Green's comments predictably brought no response at all from the committee.

I had my own questions prepared regarding the trumped up allegation. I had waited a long time to address Timms and Brown face to face and it was to be my only chance of confronting them. I was bitterly disappointed when neither was present at the meeting. The same went for Bob Turnbull, who I had intended to ask about his motive in approaching Brown to change his story after Brown had already denied making any allegation. It was unlikely I would have received answers but I had hoped at least to ask the questions.

June, who from personal experience was now fully

versed on disciplinary matters, decided to ask the committee why (contrary to Club Procedures) they had not given me prior warning of the Disciplinary Hearing or the allegation Timms intended to make. The question had barely left her lips when Ted Laycock, who had been a committee member at that meeting, instantly leapt to his feet and shot across the room yelling at June *"You shut your mouth and sit down, you've already had enough to say."* Such a display of charm and eloquence from a former Captain and President of the Club: Fortunately his outburst was met with immediate calls of 'out of order' from the general members. Alas there was no such comment from Bruce Oakes who was chairing the meeting.

It was a perfectly legitimate question but due to Laycock's outburst June never received an answer. Laycock knew the rules he was so fond of quoting didn't apply to him. He could be as offensive and ill-mannered as he wished without fear of reprimand, despite the number of witnesses to his uncivilized outburst. As with Garry Revitt, who branded June disgraceful in front of our son and other members, for making a reasonable suggestion. John Hall and others had also escaped accountability for serious breaches of the rules. Their conduct had gone completely unpunished (unlike June of course, suspended for no real reason or Ricky, who must surely be the first member of any club to face a charge of allegedly staring at someone.)

There had been a light snowfall and Revitt was prompting Oakes to close down the meeting and get on with counting the voting slips, though I have to confess the President didn't take much persuading. If the last EGM was the shortest on record this must have come a close second but ultimately it made no difference. The result of the voting was 67 votes in my favour and 212 for the committee. The number of proxy votes returned for the President was not made public. Approximately 120 members had turned up for the meeting, this left somewhere in the region of 160 votes in total being returned via proxy. These would have been registered 48 hours prior to the meeting. Accepting that (as a non member) any proxy votes returned directly in my favour would automatically be disallowed, it would seem this placed the committee in the somewhat privileged position of knowing they had passed the winning post before the race began.

In all honesty, taking account of the extended delays and the manner in which the dispute had been presented to the members, I was surprised to have received what amounted to just over half of the votes from members attending on the night and I would like to thank each member who gave me their support.

# Chapter 11

# JACK'S BACK

Following the EGM to ratify my expulsion there was nothing more to be done. Timms and the all powerful committee had won. I felt extremely sorry for my wife and son, who had been determined to do everything they possibly could to obtain justice for me and in doing so, had themselves suffered just as cruel if not a worse injustice in their attempt. I felt extremely sorry for all those who had battled on my behalf.

The committee had finally got me out of the club and out of their hair and based on the most shameful smear campaign, had also tarnished the reputation of both my wife and son, leaving them with no credibility in the club. The message emanating from the committee was one of 'moving on and at all costs preserving the harmony and ambience of the club'. The obvious implication was that in defending ourselves from the spurious allegations of others, we as a family had caused the disharmony rather than those who had made the allegations.

Throughout my dealings with the committee Peter Gleadall had been one of my staunchest supporters. In my absence he had gone on to battle on behalf of my wife and my son Ricky. In the weeks following my expulsion, Peter was shocked when the committee followed up on the most trivial catalogue of complaints by the Captain. He saw for himself how letters and witness statements from members who did not support Revitt's claims, were simply disregarded. He was especially concerned by the introduction of the new bylaw, which was promptly made good use of by immediately suspending June without any justifiable reason. No one else in the club would have been subjected to such obvious discrimination.

Peter has already been mentioned in this story, in particular with reference to letters he sent to the committee regarding the flaunting of building regulations in connection with the Stubbing Lane land and as you might gather, he did not top the list of the committee's favourite members. It seems that just when you think there are no further depths to which they can sink, certain people manage to prove you wrong.

You may recall that Peter had been a past committee member himself and as house chairman had been more than happy to do all he could for the benefit of the club, although by the time of his run-in with the Management Committee he was no longer a member of that fine league of gentlemen.

It was during Jack Timms' term of office as Club President that it was decided to make some significant alterations to the golf course. Primarily the planned works were to completely replace and relocate the existing 4th hole and in addition to re-site and build a new green to the 5th. The President, Mr Timms was in charge of the project, hiring contractors to undertake the work.

Jack Timms was no longer a member of the elite committee but as you will have gathered throughout this story, he still wealds a lot of power within the Club. In any event a few days after the EGM to ratify my expulsion, Timms approached Peter Gleadall in the club and proceeded to accuse him of having made allegations to other members that he was corrupt. This was apparently in connection with works being carried out on the golf course. He even went so far as to claim that Peter had been heard to say that Timms had taken a backhander of £20,000 in connection with the construction of the new hole. Peter was completely flabbergasted by this accusation. True to past form, Timms was not willing to divulge the source of his information but the offending remarks had allegedly taken place in the men's bar a few days earlier, on January 30th and Timms advised Gleadall that he intended to lodge an official complaint with the committee.

Peter was furious. It was inconceivable that he too was now in a similar position to me. The great man had spoken and despite the fact there was no truth to the allegation, if past experience was anything to go by, one word from Timms would be enough to start the wheels spinning into motion. It was like a recurring bad dream. The circumstances were slightly different in that Timms had been President when he made a similar allegation against me. There had been no pre-amble then, the first I had known about the charges against me was when I stood before the full committee and Timms made the unfounded allegation that ultimately lead to my eventual expulsion.

Peter Gleadall is a man with a basic sense of right and wrong, unfamiliar with those who pull the strings at Hillsborough. He is not the kind to sacrifice his integrity in order to curry favour with those full of their own self-importance and refuses to be intimidated or browbeaten. Having tirelessly supported me and my family, it seemed too much of a coincidence that he should now be next in the firing line. He gave the matter careful consideration before sending a letter to the club, addressing it to the Secretary, Thomas Pigott. Peter explained the circumstances of the allegation made by Timms and also confirmed that on the date in question (the 30th January) he recalled there having been five people present in the men's room who could all verify that he had not made any such remarks.

Gleadall resented being put in the position of having to defend himself when he had done nothing wrong and requested Pigott to inform Timms of the following:

> *"I would appreciate you writing or telling him that I state categorically that I have never discussed Jack Timms or his business affairs with any club members.*
>
> *I resent the fact that a member can be approached with a supposed allegation on hearsay from mischief makers without the member first finding out the correct facts. I felt the need to put my complaint in writing due to what has happened in the past based on just hearsay.*
>
> *Yours sincerely*
> *Peter Gleadall"*

On 18th February 2003 the Secretary replied. It was certainly not the reply Peter expected. For one thing he was reprimanded by Pigott for the time delay between writing and delivering his letter. Peter was astonished:

*"Dear Mr. Gleadall*

*Reference your letter dated 5th February 2003 received on 17th February 2003.*

*The Management Committee have instructed me to inform you that they are aware of this alleged incident and have already received a letter dated 14th February 2003 from Jack Timms.*

*The alleged remark made in the men's bar on the 30th January 2003 which was passed on to Mr. Timms was as follows :-*

- *You remarked in the presence of other members that Mr. Timms had received considerable monies from the contractors whilst handling the golf course alterations on the 4th & 5th.*

*Now you have been informed of the nature of the alleged comment would you please supply by letter your version of events on the 30th January 2003. Please include the names of the five members, who you say were present and can verify your version of the alleged incident. I have been instructed to ask these members for their version of events and report back to the Management Committee for them to decide further action if any.*

*You may if you so wish attend a meeting with the Secretary and a nominated member of the Management Committee, where you may also invite a fellow member of the club to accompany you at this meeting.*

*I trust you realise that the Management Committee*

226

*can neither reply to Mr. Timms or yourself on this matter until the facts are available.*

*I see from your letter there is a twelve day gap from the dating of the letter to the day it was received. I must stress that an immediate response to this letter is required in order to bring this matter to a conclusion as soon as possible.*

*Yours sincerely*

*T.C. Pigott*
*Honorary Secretary"*

Peter was disgusted with Pigott's letter. There was no 'version of events', Peter had already categorically stated that he had made no such remark and with the absence of any proof (other than the alleged word of Timms' faceless informant) he expected that his word would be accepted. Having been instructed by the Honorary Secretary to make an immediate response, Peter had no intention at all of ignoring such a 'polite request'. It didn't take him any time at all to consider his reply to Pigott.

*"The Secretary*
*Hillsborough Golf Club*

*19th February 2003*

*Dear Mr. Pigott*

*In reply to your letter dated 18th February 2003 regarding a letter you received from Mr. Timms dated 14th February, concerning an alleged remark that it stated I made on 30th January. A span of 14 days elapsed during the so-called remark being made and Mr. Timms reporting the complaint to you.*

*Your letter said the "Management Committee" instructed you to reply to my letter the day after you received it.*

*I find it amazing that in one day the full committee have instructed you to write to me. I believe the next full Management Committee does not take place until Monday 24th February?*

*You remark that I can attend a meeting with the Hon. Secretary (yourself) and a member of the Committee. There is a sense of deja`vu about this issue. It seems that every time people come to you with "alleged hearsay remarks that you, the Hon. Secretary want to be involved".*

*It also gives me concern that on this fact alone you state in your letter, I quote <u>That I remarked in the presence of other members that Mr. Timms etc. etc. I</u> emphatically denied making such a remark. Why was my word not believed? I am neither a liar nor a charlatan. I resent very much that I have been placed in this disgusting, embarrassing position.*

*In addition you requested the names of the other members present on that so-called occasion. If such a remark was made and I doubt it surely Mr. Timms can supply you with the names of the members from the same person whom I presume passed on this false information. The same members he wishes to have at your usual "inquisition sessions". My letter to you clearly stated that <u>"I had made no such remark".</u>*

*I would like to address the Management Committee to make a complaint of the accusation*

*made against me by Mr. Timms. I would want Mr.
Timms and his informant present please. I am
seriously considering taking legal advice against
Mr. Timms and his accusation against my good
name, reputation and exemplary character.*

*What is happening at our once friendly golf club is
unbelievable.*

*Yours faithfully
Peter Gleadall"*

It was incredible, bearing in mind the history of what
had already happened, that Pigott should pursue another
allegation based on the word of Jack Timms and his
'alleged informant'. Peter Gleadall was a highly
respected member with an exemplary record of 35 years
and he had already stated that the allegation was untrue.

The Secretary, before proceeding with the complaint,
surely had a duty to insist that Timms ask this
'anonymous informant' to come out of the shadows and
put his allegation in writing. This was the very least
Gleadall was entitled to expect. Why at Hillsborough
Golf Club did everything have to be such a cloak and
dagger affair? If Timms or indeed Pigott had proof of the
allegation made, why not be open and above board and
name the 'alleged informant'. Peter knew the allegation
against him could not be proved because he had not
made the remarks.

Peter's comment of *"there is a sense of deja` vu
about this issue"* was perfectly true.

On 26th February meanwhile Pigott replied:

*"Dear Mr. Gleadall*

*In reply to your letter dated 19th February 2003.*

*All correspondence relating to this alleged incident was discussed at the Management Committee meeting on Monday 24th February 2003.*

*The Management Committee had instructed me to inform you of the following.*

*The Honorary Secretary has standing instructions from them to deal with any complaints from members as per the Club's procedures.*

*The Club's procedure states that the Secretary and a nominated committee member would process the initial investigation regarding complaints from a member.*

*The Management Committee takes exception to your remark "inquisition sessions", as any member deserves to have an alleged complaint thoroughly investigated before any further action is taken.*

*Therefore the Secretary will continue to look into these matters and report back to the Management Committee as soon as possible.*

*Yours sincerely*

*T.C. Pigott*
*Honorary Secretary"*

So there we have it! *"The Honorary Secretary has standing instructions to deal with any complaints from members as per the Club's procedures".* What a joke! Every Club Procedure was completely disregarded when

Timms dealt with his own complaint of me and what of Pigott's dreadful handling of the Revitt's complaints of my wife June; Club Procedures were certainly not followed then. (Facts and witness statements, even the recommendation from the Ladies Committee were all ignored in favour of _the balance of probabilities, surrounding circumstances and antecedents.)_

Pigott blatantly disregarded every written request June made that procedures should be followed. He insisted contrary to the rules that she face a panel of the Management Committee (which he of course conducted) even though the Club's Procedures clearly state that all complaints against a lady member must be dealt with by the Ladies Committee.

It was courtesy of their speedily introduced new bylaw, that she was suspended without reason or proof of wrongdoing, she was not allowed any form of appeal and Pigott so rudely dismissed her numerous written requests for a copy of the taped recording of their meeting; after giving his personal assurance that she would receive one. She was treated appallingly. In fact Mr Pigott the Rules of Procedure, which you admit to writing, aren't worth the paper they are written on, except of course as now when it suits your own purpose to quote them.

I trust the reader will forgive my righteous indignation but it is downright insulting to have Pigott quote his rules to others whilst blatantly ignoring them himself.

Another priceless quote from Pigott's letter _"any member deserves to have an alleged complaint thoroughly investigated before any further action is taken"_. My complaint of Timms was not investigated.

There was no inquisition session for him? Perhaps this was because my complaint was based on fact and supported by signed witness statements, not unfounded allegations, hearsay or faceless informants.

Meanwhile the keeper of the rule book adapted to suit the occasion wrote as follows:

*"19th March 2003*

*Dear Mr. Gleadall*

*Further to the Clubs letter to you dated 26th February 2003.*

*The Management Committee have instructed me to inform you that after a preliminary investigation into this complaint, they found that there was no sound foundation to the information passed onto Mr. Timms and therefore confirm that they now consider the matter closed.*

*Mr. Timms will be informed of the Management Committee's decision.*

*The Management Committee wish to point out that although situations such as this are unpleasant for all concerned, it is essential to gather as much information as possible to enable them to reach a decision on any alleged complaint against a member.*

*Yours sincerely*

*T. C. Pigott*
*Secretary"*

What complete hogwash…. who did Pigott think he was kidding? This matter had not been unpleasant for all concerned, only for Peter Gleadall, whose word was not good enough. Don't worry Peter, if necessary Timms could probably corroborate his own complaint. What a pathetic state of affairs.

After the EGM the committee had been quick to spread their message of moving on, preserving the ambience and harmony and so forth but with one snap of his fingers, Timms again had them jumping through hoops; the target on this occasion, a man who had unfalteringly given support to me, my wife and my son Ricky.

Pigott had pronounced the matter closed but why should it be closed? There had been no explanation or apology to Gleadall and his written request to have the false allegation by Timms and his 'nameless informant' addressed by the Management Committee had simply been ignored. What sudden phenomenon had occurred to change Pigott's standing instructions that *"any member deserves to have an alleged complaint thoroughly investigated"* Did one man have sole power to decide which members did or did not deserve this right?

Pigott refused to name Timms' alleged informant and there was no investigation, no reprimand and certainly no suspension for either this anonymous person or Timms. There is something radically wrong with an organisation which tolerates the abuse of power to discriminate against and persecute certain members whilst protecting and covering up for others.

For 35 years Peter has been proud to be a member of Hillsborough Golf Club but following the events of the past couple of years that pride has gradually eroded. No matter how justified Peter's complaint of Timms was, if he pursued the matter then the committee 'courtesy of their new bylaw' now had the power to suspend him without reason as they had June. In his absence they could simply brand him and anyone else they saw fit as a troublemaker causing disharmony to the ambience etc. etc… and what could any ordinary member do - write to the committee? Peter had already witnessed what could happen. His only possible chance to change things as he saw it was to put his name up for the forthcoming committee elections at the AGM, due to take place the following month.

Four current committee men were due to stand down having completed their term of office but their names were promptly submitted for re-election. As well as the committee regulars, several rank and file members including Peter Gleadall decided to stand. There were three vacancies to be filled and (by virtue of the same method of obtaining proxy votes as at the EGM) the President was able to obtain sufficient votes to ensure the return of the three retiring committee members, only Revitt was sacrificed. All I can say is that Garry Revitt must have done something seriously wrong in vote master Oakes' eyes to lose his position. I on the other hand felt no sympathy for him at all. Peter unfortunately was unable to make any inroads into the 'closed shop syndrome'. The only change to the committee was the new Vice Captain, selected by former Captains. Promises were made that the number of proxy votes received by the President would be published for all members to see. Oddly enough this never happened so Peter Gleadall asked Thomas Pigott in person, he still awaits a response.

In 2004, the committee finally reverted to the traditional system, whereby applications for proxy forms are made in person to the Secretary of the Club. One other change was made at the same time however, concerning the retiring Past Captain and Past President, who in future may automatically remain on committee for a further year. Bruce Oakes was now entering his fifth year in office, including his year as Vice President (a situation I believe unheard of since the war.) Oakes' successor as President by the way is to be none other than Thomas Pigott. For the time being Pigott remains as Honorary Secretary as well as that of Vice President. We have yet to learn who will replace Thomas as secretary of the Club. One thing is certain! It will take a very special kind of person to fill his shoes.

On the other side of the spectrum we have people like Martin Wilkes, a man of character and integrity, who has so eloquently spoken on my behalf and supported me throughout my ordeal. He had not previously been a friend of mine; in fact I had never met him until he approached me on hearing of my problems with Hillsborough. The amount of time and effort he has put in for my cause is truly amazing. I did not ask him to help; he just volunteered and always gave it his best shot.

Martin however has finally decided he can no longer bear to be associated with the kind of people who run the show at Hillsborough. He simply cannot comprehend how Timms has been allowed to violate every rule in the book and get away with it. Hillsborough Golf Club has become a place run by people for whom Martin has no respect or regard. He cannot envisage any foreseeable change on the horizon so sadly has decided to submit his resignation. Another good man Hillsborough has lost but then who can blame him?

Throughout the course of the dispute between Hillsborough Golf Club and me, I have learned who my real friends are and also those, who when the time came to stand up and be counted simply could not do so. I have also found that there are certain people, when told to do something by a golf club committee just do it whether it is right or wrong. People who are influenced by a badge or a title and those who allow themselves to be swayed by others and are afraid to rock the boat are the people I have no time for.

There are those on the other side of the coin however and I have come to appreciate the true friendship of people like Martin, Peter, Derek Pinning and others who have had the courage to stand up and say 'this is wrong'. They did not have to, I did not ask them to; they did it because they have guts and the courage of their convictions. They have a backbone as opposed to rubber spines. They could see what was happening to me at Hillsborough and were prepared to back me despite knowing that the committee could decide to turn on them once they had finished with me. (This as you have seen is precisely what happened in the case of Peter Gleadall.) These people are my true friends and I will be eternally grateful to them.

Peter's wife Jean is out of the same mould, she is not a

golfer but like Peter she cannot tolerate injustice. Jean is a source of inspiration to anyone in need of help and support and has been a true friend to both June and I when we were most in need of one. These are the people I admire tremendously. They are what I would describe as real people. They are not shallow or superficial. They don't pretend to be your friends and then turn their back on you when the going gets tough. Possibly the only silver lining to this whole affair can be found in the people like these and others, who without any thought for their own welfare have supported me and my family simply because they know the difference between right and wrong.

I especially appreciate the help of my brother Tony and his wife Anne, whose position I realise has not been easy, also my son Russell for his patience and good humour; Norman Cinnamond, who has always been there with his friendship, encouragement and support, as have Mick Byrne, Sheila Hattersley, Pat Woodland and numerous others not mentioned by name, but whose efforts and support have certainly not been forgotten.

My special thanks go to Ray Illingworth C.B.E., who after reading my story was kind enough to write a foreward to the book. Finally, I should like to add to my list of thanks Kathryn van Gelder and Mr Price of David Price, Solicitors and Advocates of Fleet Street, for their courtesy and assistance in guiding me through the legal aspects of the book.

Since being expelled I feel I have lived under a cloud. My life and outlook have changed. People I come into contact with constantly ask the obvious questions –

how's the golf; still at Hillsborough? They mean no offence but I can't explain myself to everyone so I simply tell them the truth. *"No"* I say, *"I was expelled."* How do you justify what has happened in a few words, you can't. As things stand membership elsewhere is not an option; the first question would naturally rest on why I left Hillsborough. Again there would be no point in not being perfectly honest and having already been expelled from one Golf Club does not make me, or my family prime candidates to join another. Certain members of most Sheffield Clubs will have heard one version or another of why I was expelled. The golfing world is small and with each Club holding invitation and open days as well as inter-club friendlys; news spreads quickly, especially bad news. In short until we clear our name as a family, I feel we carry a stigma in the golfing world.

I get on with life but it has not been easy. Golf, both the game and the social side was a big part of my life and now that has all but gone. My wife and my son Ricky are for the moment still club members but they realise there is no real long term future for them at Hillsborough and they, like Martin, feel only contempt and disgust for those who have covered up for others at our expense and still continue as though nothing has happened. We no longer have the pleasure of playing golf together as a family as we once did and we obviously still miss that.

My main motivation in writing this book has been to clear our name and to validate the efforts of others who have done their very best to see justice done and in doing so have paid a price themselves. I felt compelled to expose the catalogue of shameful behaviour, especially towards my wife and son, who have not committed any crime and yet have been treated like criminals. They have undergone a terrible experience and I want others to know the injustice that has been done and the price my family and I have paid in order that others in a more privileged position could maintain their own standing in a Golf Club and in society.

# Epilogue

Before my experience at Hillsborough I genuinely believed that we were all simply members of the same club, with the same rights and responsibilities – that is to act in the best interest of the Club and to be treated equally.

It was obviously not the original intention but a two tier system seems to have evolved at Hillsborough Golf Club. We have seen how the cronyism of a one for all and all for one mentality amongst some club officials has led to a situation that neither my family, nor anyone else for that matter, should ever have to go through and I feel nothing but contempt for those who have used and abused their position of trust. Some members have suggested that perhaps HGC should follow the lead of other clubs, where the President and Captain are democratically selected by the members and if adopted this may be a welcome step forward.

A terrible injustice has happened and in writing this story I hope to have gone some way towards setting the record straight and in doing so, my family and I may finally (to coin a popular phrase of the HGC Committee) have the opportunity of 'moving on'.